FAR/AIM 2025

Last Federal Aviation Regulations/Aeronautical with Practical Exercises Operational Guidelines and Regulations for Secure Flight Navigation, Pilot's Bill of Rights, FAR/AIM Index

Easy Edu Publishing

Table of Contents

Chapter 1: Introduction to FAR

The Federal Aviation Regulations (FAR) and the Aeronautical Information Manual (AIM) collectively form the cornerstone of aviation law and operational knowledge in the United States. These documents are not merely guidelines but are legal requirements and informational resources that govern all aspects of civil aviation within the country. The FAR, part of Title 14 of the Code of Federal Regulations (CFR), is divided into sections that address various components of air travel and aviation management, including pilot certification, aircraft operation standards, and maintenance protocols. The AIM, on the other hand, provides comprehensive information on navigating the National Airspace System (NAS), effectively complementing the regulatory directives of the FAR with practical operational guidance.

Understanding the FAR/AIM is crucial for anyone involved in the aviation industry, from pilots and flight instructors to air traffic controllers and maintenance technicians. These documents ensure that all aviation activities are conducted within the bounds of safety, efficiency, and legal compliance. The FAR/AIM encompasses a wide array of topics, each meticulously detailed to address the complexities of modern aviation. These range from general operating rules, pilot certification standards, and aircraft maintenance requirements to specific operational procedures like airspace classification, navigation aids, and emergency protocols.

For pilots, the FAR/AIM is an indispensable resource. It not only outlines the legal requirements for certification and operation but also provides essential information on flight rules under various conditions, such as Visual Flight Rules (VFR) and Instrument Flight Rules (IFR). These rules are critical for safe navigation and operation within the NAS, ensuring that pilots can make informed decisions in both routine and unforeseen circumstances. Additionally, the FAR/AIM addresses critical safety topics, including alcohol and drug regulations, pilot in command responsibilities, and collision avoidance techniques, underscoring the FAA's commitment to maintaining the highest standards of air safety.

Aircraft maintenance is another area extensively covered in the FAR/AIM. The regulations stipulate the necessary inspections, preventive maintenance, and record-keeping requirements to ensure that aircraft remain safe and airworthy. These guidelines are vital for maintenance personnel, providing a clear framework for the upkeep and certification of aircraft components and systems.

The AIM further complements the FAR by offering detailed insights into airspace classification, navigation aids, and air traffic control (ATC) services. This information is crucial for both pilots and ATC personnel, facilitating efficient and safe flight operations within the complex NAS. The AIM's guidance on emergency procedures also plays a vital role in preparing aviation professionals to handle various contingencies, enhancing the overall safety of air travel.

In summary, the FAR/AIM is an essential resource for the aviation community, providing the legal, operational, and safety guidelines necessary for the conduct of civil aviation activities in the United States. Its comprehensive coverage of aviation regulations and procedures makes it an invaluable tool for ensuring safe, efficient, and compliant flight operations. As the aviation industry continues to evolve, the FAR/AIM will remain a fundamental resource, guiding the next generation of aviation professionals in their pursuit of excellence in air travel and safety.

Understanding the FAR/AIM

The Federal Aviation Regulations (FAR) and the Aeronautical Information Manual (AIM) serve as the backbone for aviation operations and safety in the United States, establishing a comprehensive framework that governs the intricacies of air navigation and management. Delving into the FAR/AIM requires a meticulous approach, given its breadth and depth covering various facets of aviation law, operational standards, and safety protocols. This exploration begins with an understanding of the FAR, which is systematically organized into parts, each dedicated to specific areas such as pilot certification, aircraft operations, and maintenance requirements. These regulations are legally enforceable and designed to ensure that all aviation activities adhere to the highest standards of safety and efficiency.

The AIM, while not regulatory, complements the FAR by providing detailed operational guidance, procedural information, and best practices to support safe and efficient flight operations. It includes vital information on airspace classification, navigation procedures, and air traffic control services, offering a practical perspective on navigating the complexities of the National Airspace System (NAS). The AIM's role is crucial in bridging the gap between regulatory mandates and real-world aviation operations, facilitating a better understanding of how to apply these regulations in various flying conditions and scenarios.

To effectively navigate the FAR/AIM, it is essential to grasp the structure and purpose of these documents. The FAR is divided into sections known as parts, with each part addressing a distinct aspect of aviation. For instance, Part 61 details the requirements for obtaining pilot certificates and ratings, while Part 91 governs general operating and flight rules. Understanding the organization of the FAR enables individuals to locate relevant regulations efficiently, a skill that is indispensable for pilots, maintenance technicians, and other aviation professionals.

Similarly, the AIM is organized into chapters and sections that systematically cover information on airspace, air navigation, and flight procedures. Its content is regularly updated to reflect the latest operational practices and technological advancements, ensuring that aviation professionals have access to current and comprehensive guidance. The AIM's emphasis on practical application makes it an invaluable resource for understanding the operational implications of the FAR and enhancing the safety and efficiency of flight operations.

Engaging with the FAR/AIM requires a proactive approach to learning and application. Aviation professionals must not only familiarize themselves with the content of these documents but also understand how to interpret and apply the regulations and guidelines to real-world situations. This involves a continuous process of education and training, as the FAR/AIM is subject to amendments and updates that reflect changes in technology, safety practices, and regulatory requirements. Staying abreast of these changes is crucial for maintaining compliance and ensuring the highest levels of safety in aviation operations.

The significance of the FAR/AIM extends beyond regulatory compliance and operational efficiency. It embodies the collective wisdom and experience of the aviation community, encapsulating lessons learned from decades of aviation operations and advancements. As such, the FAR/AIM is not merely a set of rules and guidelines but a dynamic framework that supports the ongoing development and safety of the aviation industry. Engaging with these documents is a fundamental responsibility for all members of the aviation community, from pilots and air traffic controllers to maintenance personnel and aviation administrators.

Through diligent study and application of the FAR/AIM, aviation professionals can navigate the complexities of the regulatory environment with confidence. This requires not only an understanding of the letter of the law but also an appreciation for its intent and practical application in daily operations. For example, while the FAR outlines the minimum legal requirements for aircraft maintenance, the AIM provides additional context and best practices that can help maintenance personnel exceed these standards, thereby enhancing aircraft safety and reliability.

The process of interpreting the FAR/AIM can be challenging, given the technical nature of the documents and the legal language used. However, several strategies can facilitate a deeper understanding. Firstly, cross-referencing between the FAR and the AIM can provide a more holistic view of a topic, as the regulatory requirements are often expanded upon with practical guidance in the AIM. Additionally, utilizing resources such as FAA advisory circulars, which offer explanations and recommendations for complying with the FAR, can provide clarity and assist in the application of complex regulations.

Another critical aspect of engaging with the FAR/AIM is the need for critical thinking and judgment. Aviation professionals must be able to assess situations and make informed decisions based on a comprehensive understanding of the regulations and their operational context. This is particularly important in scenarios not explicitly covered by the regulations, where the principles and safety considerations outlined in the FAR/AIM must guide decision-making.

The FAR/AIM also plays a pivotal role in training and education within the aviation industry. Flight instructors, for example, rely heavily on these documents to structure their lessons and ensure that students are not only prepared to pass their certification exams but also to operate safely and effectively in the real world. Similarly, aviation maintenance training programs incorporate the FAR/AIM to ensure that technicians are fully aware of the legal requirements for aircraft upkeep and are equipped to perform their duties to the highest standards.

In addition to individual study and application, discussions and collaborations among aviation professionals can enhance understanding and interpretation of the FAR/AIM. Forums, workshops, and professional associations provide opportunities for sharing insights, asking questions, and learning from the experiences of others. These interactions can uncover practical tips for compliance, innovative approaches to common challenges, and a deeper appreciation for the rationale behind certain regulations.

Ultimately, the FAR/AIM is a living document that evolves in response to the needs of the aviation industry, technological advancements, and lessons learned from operational experiences. Active engagement with these documents is essential for staying current with regulatory changes and maintaining the safety, efficiency, and legality of aviation operations. By approaching the FAR/AIM with a commitment to continuous learning and professional development, aviation professionals can contribute to the advancement of the industry and uphold the highest standards of air safety and operational excellence.

The Importance of Compliance

Compliance with Federal Aviation Regulations (FAR) and adherence to the Aeronautical Information Manual (AIM) is not merely a legal obligation but a cornerstone of aviation safety, efficiency, and professionalism. The intricate fabric of the aviation sector is held together by these regulations and guidelines, ensuring that all operations, from individual flights to comprehensive air traffic management, meet the highest standards of safety and operational integrity. Compliance serves as the foundation upon which trust between the public, the aviation industry, and regulatory bodies is built and maintained. It is a critical element in the prevention of accidents and incidents, safeguarding not only those who navigate the skies but also individuals on the ground.

The FAR/AIM encompasses a broad spectrum of aviation activities, including pilot certification, aircraft maintenance, and air traffic control operations. Each regulation and guideline is the result of extensive research, expert input, and lessons learned from past experiences. Therefore, adherence to these standards is not optional but mandatory for all aviation professionals and entities. Compliance ensures that pilots possess the requisite skills and knowledge, aircraft are maintained in an airworthy condition, and air traffic is managed to mitigate risks of collision and other hazards.

The legal implications of non-compliance can be severe, ranging from fines and suspension of licenses to criminal charges in cases of gross negligence. However, the consequences extend beyond legal penalties. Non-compliance can lead to accidents that result in loss of life, significant financial losses for operators, and damage to the reputation of involved parties. Moreover, it can erode public confidence in the aviation system, which is detrimental to the industry as a whole.

To achieve compliance, aviation professionals must engage in continuous learning and professional development. The FAR/AIM is subject to regular updates and amendments, reflecting changes in technology, operational practices, and safety protocols. Staying informed of these changes is essential. Aviation professionals should utilize available resources, including FAA advisories, training programs, and industry seminars, to keep their knowledge and skills current.

In addition to individual efforts, organizations within the aviation industry play a crucial role in promoting compliance. This includes implementing robust safety management systems, conducting regular audits and inspections, and fostering a culture of safety and compliance. Organizations should provide their employees with the necessary tools, training, and support to understand and adhere to the FAR/AIM. Encouraging open communication about safety concerns and potential regulatory violations without fear of retribution is also vital.

Compliance with the FAR/AIM is a shared responsibility among all stakeholders in the aviation industry. It requires a proactive approach to understanding and applying the regulations and guidelines in every aspect of aviation operations. By prioritizing compliance, the aviation community can continue to advance the safety, efficiency, and reliability of air travel. This collective commitment to upholding the standards set forth in the

FAR/AIM is essential for the continued growth and development of the aviation industry, ensuring that it remains a safe and viable mode of transportation for future generations.

Chapter 2: Aircraft Operations

General Operating and Flight Rules form the bedrock of safe, efficient, and lawful aircraft operations, encompassing a wide array of regulations that govern the day-to-day activities of pilots, flight crews, and operators within the National Airspace System (NAS). These rules are meticulously designed to ensure that all aircraft operations, regardless of their nature or complexity, adhere to standardized procedures that prioritize safety and operational integrity. Among the most critical aspects of these regulations are the responsibilities of the Pilot in Command (PIC), which include but are not limited to, the ultimate responsibility for the safety of a flight, adherence to the flight plan, and compliance with all applicable regulations during the operation of the aircraft.

The Pilot in Command is vested with the authority to make pivotal decisions regarding the flight, including any alterations to the planned route or the execution of emergency procedures as circumstances dictate. This authority is complemented by a corresponding set of responsibilities, ensuring that the PIC possesses not only the requisite knowledge and skills but also a profound understanding of their legal and ethical obligations. The regulations clearly delineate these responsibilities, emphasizing the PIC's role in maintaining the highest standards of safety and compliance.

Alcohol and Drug Regulations represent another cornerstone of the General Operating and Flight Rules, underscoring the Federal Aviation Administration's (FAA) commitment to ensuring that individuals involved in the operation of aircraft are free from the impairments caused by substances. These regulations set forth strict guidelines regarding the consumption of alcohol and the use of drugs, specifying allowable limits and the requisite periods of abstinence prior to operating an aircraft. The intent behind these rules is to eliminate any potential for impairment that could compromise the safety of flight operations, reflecting a zero-tolerance policy towards substance abuse in aviation.

Flight Rules under Visual Flight Rules (VFR) and Instrument Flight Rules (IFR) provide comprehensive frameworks for the conduct of flights under varying conditions of visibility and weather. VFR operations are characterized by a reliance on visual cues for navigation and the avoidance of clouds, requiring pilots to maintain a certain degree of visibility and distance from clouds at all times. These conditions facilitate the pilot's ability to see and avoid other aircraft, thereby reducing the risk of mid-air collisions. Conversely, IFR operations allow pilots to operate in conditions of reduced visibility, relying on instrument readings for navigation and the adherence to specific air traffic control (ATC) clearances. The transition between VFR and IFR operations is governed by precise regulations that ensure pilots are adequately prepared and certified to undertake flights under either set of conditions, depending on the prevailing weather and visibility.

The intricacies of these rules highlight the FAA's multifaceted approach to regulating aircraft operations, balancing the need for flexibility in the conduct of flights with an unwavering focus on safety. Each regulation is crafted with the understanding that the dynamics of flight operations can vary significantly, necessitating a regulatory framework that is both comprehensive and adaptable. As such, the General Operating and Flight Rules serve not only as a guide for the conduct of safe and efficient flight operations but also as a testament to the FAA's commitment to upholding the highest standards of aviation safety.

Beyond the foundational aspects of Pilot in Command responsibilities and the stringent alcohol and drug regulations, the General Operating and Flight Rules delve into the specifics of flight operations under both Visual Flight Rules (VFR) and Instrument Flight Rules (IFR). These rules are essential for the safe conduct of flights, dictating how pilots should navigate the airspace under varying weather conditions and visibility. The distinction between VFR and IFR is critical, as it determines the set of regulations that a flight operation will adhere to, impacting everything from pre-flight planning to the execution of the flight itself.

VFR operations, while seemingly straightforward, require pilots to maintain a vigilant awareness of their surroundings, ensuring that they can visually navigate and avoid obstacles or other aircraft. This mode of operation is predicated on clear weather conditions and sufficient visibility, allowing pilots to operate the aircraft with visual references to the ground and other objects. The FAA stipulates specific visibility and cloud clearance requirements for VFR flights, which vary depending on the class of airspace in which the flight is conducted. These requirements are designed to minimize the risk of collisions and ensure that pilots have adequate visual reference to navigate safely.

In contrast, IFR operations allow pilots to fly in a broader range of weather conditions, including those in which visual navigation is not feasible. Pilots flying under IFR rely on aircraft instruments and navigation systems to guide them, following a predetermined route and adhering to clearances issued by air traffic control (ATC). This mode of operation necessitates a higher level of training and certification, as pilots must be adept at interpreting instrument readings and managing the aircraft without visual references to the outside world. The transition from VFR to IFR, or vice versa, is governed by specific procedures that ensure the safety of the flight and the efficiency of the airspace system.

The FAA's regulations also encompass special flight operations, including those conducted at night or over water, which present unique challenges and require additional considerations. Night operations, for example, necessitate the use of specific navigation and lighting equipment, while flights over water may require the carriage of life rafts and other survival gear. These regulations ensure that pilots are prepared for the specific conditions they may encounter during such operations, enhancing the overall safety of the flight.

Moreover, the General Operating and Flight Rules address the use of airspace, detailing the requirements and restrictions associated with different classes of airspace. Pilots must be familiar with the characteristics of the airspace through which they will fly, including any restrictions or requirements for entry. This knowledge is crucial for maintaining the safe and orderly flow of air traffic, preventing conflicts between aircraft, and ensuring that flights operate within the parameters set by the FAA.

In summary, the General Operating and Flight Rules provide a comprehensive framework for the conduct of safe, efficient, and lawful aircraft operations. From the foundational responsibilities of the Pilot in Command to the detailed regulations governing VFR and IFR operations, these rules encapsulate the FAA's commitment to aviation safety. Pilots, flight crews, and operators must adhere to these regulations, ensuring that every flight is conducted with the utmost regard for safety and operational integrity. Through diligent adherence to these rules, the aviation community upholds the standards of excellence and safety that define the industry, contributing to the continued development and reliability of air travel.

General Operating and Flight Rules

General Operating and Flight Rules encompass a wide range of regulations designed to ensure the safety and efficiency of flight operations within the National Airspace System (NAS). These rules are applicable to all types of aircraft, from small private planes to large commercial jets, and they cover every aspect of flight, including takeoff, cruising altitude, landing, and everything in between. The Federal Aviation Administration (FAA) has established these rules to create a standardized set of procedures and requirements that all pilots and flight operators must follow to maintain the highest levels of safety in the skies.

One of the key components of the General Operating and Flight Rules is the requirement for pre-flight planning and briefing. Pilots are required to thoroughly plan their flights, taking into consideration factors such as weather conditions, route selection, fuel requirements, and alternate airports in case of an emergency. This meticulous planning ensures that pilots are prepared for a wide range of scenarios that they may encounter during their flight. Additionally, pilots must also conduct a thorough pre-flight inspection of their aircraft to ensure that all systems are functioning correctly and that the aircraft is safe for flight.

Another critical aspect of the General Operating and Flight Rules is the adherence to established flight rules depending on the conditions of the flight. Pilots must decide whether to fly under Visual Flight Rules (VFR) or Instrument Flight Rules (IFR) based on weather conditions and their qualifications. VFR flights are typically conducted in clear weather conditions where the pilot navigates the aircraft by visual reference to the terrain. In contrast, IFR flights are conducted in poor weather conditions or above cloud layers where pilots must rely on instrument navigation to guide the aircraft. The decision between VFR and IFR significantly affects the planning and conduct of the flight, including route selection, altitude, and communication with air traffic control.

Communication with air traffic control (ATC) is another cornerstone of the General Operating and Flight Rules. Pilots must maintain constant communication with ATC when flying in controlled airspace to receive instructions for safe navigation and to ensure separation from other aircraft. This communication is vital for maintaining the orderly flow of air traffic and preventing collisions. Pilots are required to understand and use standard aviation phraseology to ensure clear and concise communication with ATC, enhancing the safety of all flight operations.

The rules also stipulate strict adherence to altitude and speed regulations. These regulations are designed to ensure that aircraft operate safely within their performance limitations and maintain adequate separation from other aircraft. Speed limitations vary depending on the type of airspace, the phase of flight, and the proximity to airports, while altitude regulations ensure that aircraft follow a safe flight path, avoiding obstacles and minimizing the risk of mid-air collisions.

Pilots are also required to be familiar with and adhere to airspace restrictions and classifications. The NAS is divided into various classes of airspace, each with its own set of entry, communication, and equipment requirements. Understanding these requirements is crucial for pilots to navigate the airspace safely and legally. Special use airspace, such as restricted areas, military operation areas (MOAs), and temporary flight restrictions (TFRs), impose additional restrictions to ensure the safety and security of flight operations. Pilots must check for any airspace restrictions along their planned route during the pre-flight briefing process and remain vigilant for any changes during the flight.

In addition to these operational rules, the General Operating and Flight Rules also cover regulations related to emergency procedures. Pilots must be proficient in handling various in-flight emergencies, including engine failures, electrical failures, and medical emergencies. The FAA provides guidelines for responding to these situations, and pilots are expected to be familiar with these procedures and capable of executing them if necessary. Emergency procedures are an essential part of pilot training and are regularly practiced to ensure that pilots can respond effectively to any situation.

The General Operating and Flight Rules form the foundation of safe and efficient flight operations in the United States. By adhering to these rules, pilots and flight operators ensure the safety of their passengers, crew, and the general public. The FAA continuously updates these regulations to reflect changes in technology, operational practices, and safety research, making it imperative for aviation professionals to stay informed of the latest developments. Through compliance with these rules, the aviation community works together to maintain the high safety standards that have made air travel one of the safest modes of transportation.

Pilot in Command Responsibilities

The Pilot in Command (PIC) bears the ultimate responsibility for the safety and operational compliance of a flight, a role enshrined in the Federal Aviation Regulations (FAR). This responsibility encompasses a broad spectrum of duties, from pre-flight planning to the execution of the flight and the decision-making processes involved in responding to in-flight emergencies. The PIC is tasked with ensuring that the aircraft is airworthy, that the flight operation complies with all applicable regulations, and that the safety of passengers and crew is maintained at all times. This includes the adherence to operational limitations and the execution of all necessary procedures to mitigate risks during flight operations.

A critical component of the PIC's responsibilities is the thorough assessment of weather conditions prior to and during the flight. This involves not only the review of meteorological reports and forecasts but also the application of this information in the decision-making process, particularly when determining the feasibility of continuing the flight as planned or the need to seek an alternate route or destination. The PIC must possess the ability to interpret weather data accurately and make informed decisions that prioritize safety above all else.

In addition to weather considerations, the PIC is responsible for ensuring that the aircraft is properly loaded and that the weight and balance of the aircraft are within the prescribed limits for safe operation. This involves the calculation and verification of load distribution and fuel requirements to ensure that the aircraft's performance will not be adversely affected during the flight. The PIC must also ensure that all necessary documentation, including the aircraft's logbooks, certificates, and any required customs, immigration, or health documents, are in order and accessible.

The PIC's authority extends to the management of the crew and passengers. This includes the delegation of duties to other crew members in a manner that ensures the efficient and safe operation of the flight. The

PIC must also ensure that passengers are briefed on safety procedures and that any passenger-related issues are managed effectively to maintain the safety and security of the flight. In the event of an in-flight emergency, the PIC has the authority to take whatever action is deemed necessary to ensure the safety of the flight, including diverting to an alternate airport or executing emergency procedures as required.

Communication is a pivotal aspect of the PIC's responsibilities. This entails maintaining effective communication with air traffic control (ATC) and ensuring that all ATC instructions are followed unless doing so would compromise the safety of the flight. The PIC must also ensure that communication within the cockpit and with cabin crew is clear and effective, facilitating a collaborative approach to flight operations and safety management.

The PIC's responsibilities also encompass compliance with all operational regulations, including airspace restrictions, speed limitations, and adherence to flight plans. This requires a comprehensive understanding of the FAR and the ability to apply these regulations in a practical context. The PIC must remain informed of any regulatory changes or temporary flight restrictions that may affect the flight and must ensure that the flight operation complies with all applicable laws and regulations.

The role of the PIC is characterized by a high degree of responsibility and authority. It demands not only technical proficiency and operational knowledge but also strong leadership and decision-making skills. The safety of the flight hinges on the PIC's ability to manage a wide range of operational, environmental, and regulatory challenges, making the role of the PIC critical to the success of every flight operation. The fulfillment of these responsibilities ensures the safety and security of air travel, underscoring the importance of the PIC in the aviation industry.

Alcohol and Drug Regulations

Federal Aviation Administration (FAA) regulations concerning alcohol and drug use among aviation personnel are stringent and non-negotiable, designed to ensure the highest levels of safety in the aviation industry. The FAA's regulations prohibit pilots, flight crew, and other safety-sensitive personnel from performing their duties with a blood alcohol content (BAC) of 0.04 percent or higher, a standard that is more stringent than those for most motor vehicle drivers. Furthermore, the rules mandate that no alcohol is to be consumed by these individuals within eight hours of performing flight duties, commonly referred to as the "bottle to throttle" rule. However, to accommodate for individual differences in alcohol metabolism, many airlines and aviation professionals adhere to a more conservative 12-hour rule.

In addition to restrictions on alcohol consumption, the FAA has established comprehensive guidelines to govern the use of drugs among aviation personnel. These regulations explicitly prohibit the use of any substance that affects the person's faculties in any way contrary to safety. This includes not only illicit drugs but also certain prescription medications and over-the-counter drugs that may impair an individual's ability to perform safety-sensitive functions. The FAA maintains a list of medications that are considered disqualifying due to their potential effects on cognitive and motor functions. Aviation personnel are required to consult with aviation medical examiners (AMEs) or other medical professionals to determine whether a particular medication is safe for use while performing flight duties.

The FAA's drug and alcohol testing program is another critical component of its efforts to maintain a drug-free workplace within the aviation industry. This program requires employers to conduct pre-employment, random, reasonable suspicion, post-accident, return-to-duty, and follow-up drug and alcohol testing of safety-sensitive employees. The testing protocols are designed to detect the presence of alcohol and specific drugs, including marijuana, cocaine, opiates, amphetamines, and phencyclidine (PCP). In the event of a positive test result, the individual is immediately removed from performing safety-sensitive duties and is subject to disciplinary actions, which may include termination of employment and revocation of FAA certificates.

The FAA also emphasizes the importance of education and training in preventing drug and alcohol abuse among aviation personnel. Employers are required to provide their employees with information about the dangers of drug and alcohol use, the details of the company's testing program, and the resources available for those seeking help with substance abuse issues. This educational component is vital in fostering a culture of safety and responsibility within the aviation community.

To ensure compliance with these regulations, the FAA conducts regular audits and inspections of airlines and other aviation entities. These oversight activities are designed to verify that proper drug and alcohol testing procedures are in place and that employees are aware of and adhering to the regulations. Non-compliance can result in significant penalties for both individuals and employers, including fines, suspension of operations, and loss of certification.

The FAA's alcohol and drug regulations are a testament to the agency's commitment to maintaining the highest standards of safety in the aviation industry. By setting clear guidelines for alcohol and drug use, enforcing strict testing protocols, and promoting education and awareness, the FAA aims to prevent substance-related incidents and accidents, ensuring the safety of passengers, crew, and the general public. Compliance with these regulations is not only a legal requirement but also a moral imperative for all aviation professionals, underscoring the collective responsibility to uphold the integrity and safety of air travel.

Flight Rules under VFR

Visual Flight Rules (VFR) are a set of regulations under which a pilot operates an aircraft in weather conditions generally clear enough to allow the pilot to see where the aircraft is going. The fundamental essence of VFR flying is that the pilot must be able to operate the aircraft with visual reference to the ground, and by visually avoiding obstructions and other aircraft. Pilots flying under VFR assume responsibility for their separation from all other aircraft and must be vigilant in observing the airspace around them to maintain situational awareness and safety. The Federal Aviation Administration (FAA) delineates specific requirements and conditions under which VFR flights must be conducted, including but not limited to visibility, cloud clearance, and specific altitudes.

Visibility requirements under VFR are paramount; pilots must adhere to minimum visibility standards which vary depending on the class of airspace in which the aircraft is operating. For instance, in controlled airspace around airports, known as Class B, C, D, and E airspace, visibility must be at least 3 miles during the day. However, in uncontrolled airspace, or Class G airspace, the minimum visibility requirement can be as low as 1 mile during the day under certain conditions. These visibility standards ensure that pilots have sufficient visual reference to navigate, avoid conflicts with other aircraft, and recognize potential hazards in their flight path.

Cloud clearance is another critical aspect of VFR flight; pilots must maintain a certain distance from clouds at all times. This distance varies by airspace class but is designed to ensure that pilots have unobstructed views of their surroundings, other aircraft, and any potential obstacles. For example, in most controlled airspaces, an aircraft must maintain a distance of 500 feet below, 1,000 feet above, and 2,000 feet horizontally from clouds. These clearances facilitate safe navigation and prevent inadvertent entry into Instrument Meteorological Conditions (IMC), which could disorient pilots and lead to loss of control of the aircraft.

Altitude regulations under VFR are established to promote safe flight operations and efficient use of airspace. When flying over congested areas or open water, pilots must maintain an altitude that would allow them to perform an emergency landing without undue hazard to persons or property on the surface in the event of a power failure. Specifically, over congested areas, the minimum altitude is 1,000 feet above the highest obstacle within a horizontal radius of 2,000 feet of the aircraft, while over uncongested areas, the minimum altitude is 500 feet above the surface.

Pilots operating under VFR must also be aware of special VFR conditions which allow flights to operate in controlled airspace with less than standard VFR weather minimums, provided they have clearance from air traffic control (ATC). This special VFR is only available during daylight hours unless the pilot and aircraft are equipped and certified for night flying. Special VFR provides flexibility in flight operations but requires pilots to exercise increased caution and vigilance due to the reduced visibility and proximity to other aircraft.

VFR navigation relies heavily on pilotage and dead reckoning, utilizing visual references on the ground, such as roads, rivers, and landmarks, to guide the flight path. While modern aircraft may be equipped with sophisticated navigation aids, the essence of VFR flying is the ability to navigate using these basic techniques, ensuring that pilots maintain a strong situational awareness of their location relative to terrain, obstacles, and other airspace users.

In summary, flying under Visual Flight Rules requires pilots to maintain a clear view of the horizon and ground at all times, ensuring safe separation from clouds, sufficient visibility, and adherence to specified altitudes. These rules are designed to ensure that pilots can see and avoid other aircraft, navigate safely using visual references, and respond promptly to any potential hazards. Compliance with VFR regulations is essential for the safety of all airspace users, and pilots must be thoroughly familiar with these requirements and prepared to apply them in their flight operations.

Flight Rules under IFR

Flight under Instrument Flight Rules (IFR) demands a comprehensive understanding of the regulations, procedures, and operational requirements to ensure safety and compliance within the National Airspace System. Pilots operating under IFR are subject to a set of rules that are fundamentally designed to govern flight operations without reliance on visual cues. These rules facilitate the safe and efficient use of airspace by establishing standardized procedures for flying in instrument meteorological conditions (IMC), where visibility is reduced, and navigation based on visual landmarks becomes impractical or impossible.

The cornerstone of IFR flight operations is the requirement for pilots to be appropriately certified and for aircraft to be properly equipped for instrument flight. The Federal Aviation Administration (FAA) mandates that pilots must hold an Instrument Rating to their Airman Certificate, which validates their proficiency in flying by instruments alone. This rating is obtained through a rigorous training and testing process that covers a broad spectrum of knowledge areas including, but not limited to, understanding of the IFR system, proficiency in instrument navigation, and the ability to interpret and respond to instrument flight data.

Aircraft used for IFR flight must meet specific equipment requirements set forth in the FARs. These requirements ensure that the aircraft is capable of performing under the demands of instrument flight, including navigation and communication under ATC directives. Equipment such as altimeters, transponders, navigation and communication radios, and, in many cases, an autopilot system, must be installed and functioning to the standards prescribed by the FAA. Regular maintenance and inspection of these systems are critical to ensuring their reliability and functionality in IFR conditions.

Air Traffic Control (ATC) plays a pivotal role in the management of IFR flights. Pilots operating under IFR are required to file a flight plan with ATC, providing detailed information about their intended route, altitude, and timing. Once in flight, pilots must adhere strictly to ATC instructions, which are designed to maintain safe separation between aircraft and to navigate them efficiently to their destinations. The interaction between pilots and ATC under IFR is governed by a structured communication protocol, which ensures clarity and precision in the exchange of information.

Understanding and adhering to the published IFR routes and procedures is essential for the safe conduct of instrument flights. The FAA publishes a vast network of airways, known as the Victor and Jet routes for lower and higher altitudes respectively, along with Standard Instrument Departures (SID) and Standard Terminal Arrival Routes (STAR), which are designed to streamline the flow of air traffic into and out of busy airspace areas. Compliance with these prescribed routes and procedures not only contributes to the safety of the flight but also enhances the efficiency of the airspace system as a whole.

Navigating under IFR requires a solid grasp of instrument navigation techniques and the use of navigational aids (NAVAIDs). Pilots must be proficient in the use of VORs (VHF Omnidirectional Range), NDBs (Non-Directional Beacons), DME (Distance Measuring Equipment), and GPS (Global Positioning System) for en-route navigation, as well as ILS (Instrument Landing System), VOR, and GPS approaches for precision and non-precision approaches to airports. The ability to interpret and apply the information from these aids is critical for maintaining the intended flight path, especially when visibility is compromised.

The transition from en-route to terminal operations under IFR involves specific procedures for approach and landing, which are designed to ensure that aircraft are aligned with the runway and descend at an appropriate rate for a safe landing. Pilots must be familiar with the various types of instrument approaches and be prepared to execute missed approach procedures if necessary.

The execution of instrument approaches requires precise timing, altitude control, and adherence to the approach procedure as outlined in the approach plates. These plates provide critical information such as minimum descent altitudes, approach course alignments, and missed approach instructions. Proficiency in reading and interpreting these plates is indispensable for IFR pilots, ensuring that they can safely navigate through the final phases of flight and land under limited visibility conditions. It is imperative for pilots to maintain situational awareness and to be prepared for rapid decision-making, especially when confronted with unexpected events such as sudden weather changes or equipment malfunctions during an approach.

Missed approach procedures are an integral part of IFR operations, designed to provide a safe alternative in the event that landing is not advisable or possible upon reaching the minimum descent altitude or decision height. Pilots must be ready to initiate a missed approach if the required visual references for the runway are not clearly visible or if instructed by ATC. This involves executing a predefined series of maneuvers to climb and navigate away from the airport, thereby ensuring the aircraft remains clear of terrain and obstacles while the pilot or ATC establishes an alternative plan for landing.

The importance of continuous communication with ATC cannot be overstated in IFR flight. From the moment of departure to the completion of an approach, pilots must maintain an open channel of communication with controllers, reporting their position, intentions, and receiving instructions or updates on flight conditions. This collaborative effort between pilots and ATC is crucial for the dynamic management of airspace and the safe coordination of flights operating under instrument conditions.

Moreover, IFR flight planning is a critical pre-flight task that requires meticulous attention to detail. Pilots must evaluate weather forecasts, NOTAMs (Notices to Airmen), and TFRs (Temporary Flight Restrictions) to ensure that the chosen route is viable and complies with all regulatory requirements. The flight plan must include considerations for fuel requirements, alternate airports, and the potential need for route adjustments due to weather or airspace restrictions. Effective flight planning mitigates risks and contributes to the overall safety and efficiency of the flight.

In summary, flying under IFR is a complex operation that demands a high level of skill, knowledge, and discipline from pilots. It encompasses a wide range of procedures and regulations designed to ensure the safety of flight operations in conditions where visual navigation is not possible. Mastery of instrument navigation techniques, thorough pre-flight planning, adherence to ATC instructions, and the ability to perform under pressure are all essential components of successful IFR flight. Through diligent study, training, and experience, pilots can achieve the proficiency required to navigate the skies safely and efficiently, regardless of visibility conditions.

Chapter 3: Airman Certification

Eligibility requirements for airman certification encompass a broad spectrum of criteria designed to ensure that candidates possess the necessary knowledge, skill, and experience to operate safely within the National Airspace System. The Federal Aviation Administration (FAA) delineates these requirements within Title 14 of the Code of Federal Regulations (CFR), specifically under parts 61 and 141, which detail the standards for obtaining various pilot certificates and ratings. Candidates seeking certification must meet age, language proficiency, medical fitness, educational background, and flight experience prerequisites, each tailored to the level of certification being pursued.

Age requirements vary by certification type; for instance, to obtain a Private Pilot Certificate, an individual must be at least 17 years old, whereas for a Commercial Pilot Certificate, the minimum age is 18. The Airline Transport Pilot Certificate, the highest level of pilot certification, requires the candidate to be at least 23 years old. These age requirements ensure that candidates have attained a level of maturity and decision-making capability essential for the responsibilities associated with each level of certification.

Language proficiency is critical for clear and effective communication within the aviation environment. The FAA mandates that candidates must be able to read, speak, write, and understand English, the international language of aviation. This requirement is fundamental for safety, facilitating unambiguous communication between pilots, air traffic controllers, and other aviation professionals.

Medical certificates are another cornerstone of the eligibility criteria, underscoring the importance of physical and mental fitness in aviation. The FAA classifies medical certificates into three categories: First-Class for airline transport pilots, Second-Class for commercial pilots, and Third-Class for student, recreational, and private pilots. Obtaining a medical certificate involves a comprehensive examination by an FAA-designated Aviation Medical Examiner (AME) to assess the candidate's health and fitness for flying. Conditions that impair cognitive function, vision, equilibrium, or cardiovascular health can disqualify an individual from receiving a medical certificate, although certain waivers or special issuances can be granted under specific circumstances.

Educational background, while not prescribed in terms of specific qualifications, plays a significant role in a candidate's ability to grasp the theoretical concepts of aviation. A solid understanding of mathematics, physics, and geography is beneficial for pilot training. However, the FAA places greater emphasis on knowledge and proficiency demonstrated through written exams, practical tests, and the ability to apply theoretical concepts in real-world flying situations.

Flight experience requirements are detailed and vary significantly across different types of certifications and ratings. For example, a Private Pilot Certificate requires a minimum of 40 hours of flight time, including 20 hours of flight training with an instructor and 10 hours of solo flight. In contrast, an Airline Transport Pilot Certificate requires at least 1,500 hours of flight time. These hours include specific conditions of flight, such as night flying, cross-country navigation, and instrument conditions, ensuring that the candidate has a well-rounded experience in various flying environments.

Candidates must pass a series of written exams that test their knowledge of FAA regulations, aerodynamics, navigation, weather, and aircraft operations specific to the certification sought. These exams are computer-based and consist of multiple-choice questions designed to assess the candidate's understanding of critical aviation topics.

Practical tests, or check rides, are the final step in the certification process, where candidates demonstrate their flying skills and decision-making abilities to an FAA-designated examiner. The practical test is conducted according to the FAA's Practical Test Standards (PTS) or Airman Certification Standards (ACS), which outline the performance criteria for various maneuvers and operational tasks. Successful completion of the practical test signifies that the candidate possesses the competence and skill to operate safely and effectively as a certified pilot.

In conclusion, the eligibility requirements for airman certification are comprehensive and designed to ensure that pilots are thoroughly prepared for the challenges of aviation. Meeting these requirements involves a combination of formal education, medical fitness, practical experience, and a demonstrated proficiency in aviation knowledge and skills. Through this rigorous certification process, the FAA upholds the safety and integrity of the National Airspace System, ensuring that pilots are capable of contributing positively to the aviation community.

Eligibility Requirements

Eligibility requirements for aspiring aviators are meticulously outlined by the Federal Aviation Administration (FAA) to ensure that individuals seeking airman certification possess the requisite knowledge, skills, and experience to operate safely within the National Airspace System. These criteria serve as a foundational pillar in the FAA's commitment to maintaining the highest standards of aviation safety and operational integrity. Prospective pilots must navigate a series of regulatory prerequisites, each designed to rigorously assess their readiness for the responsibilities that accompany pilot certification.

Age and language proficiency constitute the initial barriers to entry for candidates. The FAA mandates specific age requirements for each category of pilot certification, reflecting the progressive levels of responsibility and expertise required. For instance, the minimum age for obtaining a Private Pilot Certificate is 17 years, ensuring that candidates have reached a level of maturity conducive to managing the complexities of piloting an aircraft. Similarly, the requirement for proficiency in English, the international language of aviation, underscores the critical importance of clear and effective communication in flight operations and air traffic control interactions.

The medical fitness of candidates is rigorously evaluated through a structured examination process conducted by FAA-designated Aviation Medical Examiners. This assessment is pivotal in identifying any physical or mental conditions that could impair a pilot's ability to safely operate an aircraft. The classification of medical certificates into First, Second, and Third-Class reflects the varying degrees of medical scrutiny aligned with the specific demands of different pilot certifications. The integrity of this medical certification process is a cornerstone of the FAA's safety oversight, ensuring that pilots meet stringent health and fitness standards.

Educational background, while not prescribed in specific terms, plays an instrumental role in a candidate's ability to comprehend and apply the complex theoretical concepts fundamental to aviation. The FAA's emphasis on demonstrated knowledge and proficiency, rather than formal educational qualifications, allows for a diverse range of individuals to pursue pilot certification. This approach facilitates access to aviation careers while maintaining the rigorous standards necessary for safe flight operations.

Flight experience requirements are precisely defined, with detailed stipulations regarding the minimum hours of flight time, the nature of the flying experience, and the conditions under which it must be obtained. These requirements are tailored to ensure that candidates have acquired a comprehensive and practical understanding of flight operations across a spectrum of conditions and scenarios. The FAA's specification of flight experience criteria is designed to cultivate well-rounded aviators capable of navigating the complexities of the National Airspace System with skill and confidence.

The FAA's written exams and practical tests are critical components of the certification process, designed to rigorously evaluate a candidate's theoretical knowledge and practical flying skills. The computer-based written exams test a wide range of aviation-related knowledge, from FAA regulations to aerodynamics and navigation. The practical tests, or check rides, conducted under the scrutiny of FAA-designated examiners, are the culmination of the certification process, where candidates must demonstrate their flying proficiency and decision-making abilities in real-world scenarios. These assessments ensure that only those individuals who meet the FAA's exacting standards are granted pilot certification.

The eligibility requirements for airman certification are comprehensive and multifaceted, reflecting the FAA's unwavering commitment to aviation safety. Through this rigorous certification process, the FAA ensures that pilots possess not only the technical knowledge and practical skills necessary for safe flight operations but also the judgment and decision-making capabilities essential for navigating the dynamic and often challenging environment of the National Airspace System. The structured framework of these requirements serves to uphold the safety, efficiency, and integrity of aviation, fostering a culture of excellence among pilots and contributing to the overall safety of the aviation community.

Age and Language

Age and language proficiency are pivotal eligibility criteria for airman certification, ensuring candidates possess the maturity and communication skills essential for aviation safety. The Federal Aviation Administration (FAA) sets specific age requirements for different levels of pilot certification to ensure that individuals have reached a developmental stage where they can responsibly manage the complexities and demands of operating an aircraft. For instance, the minimum age to obtain a Private Pilot Certificate is 17 years, reflecting the FAA's assessment of the maturity required to undertake pilot training and responsibilities. This age criterion escalates for more advanced certifications, with the Airline Transport Pilot Certificate requiring candidates to be at least 23 years old, acknowledging the greater responsibility and experience needed at this level.

Language proficiency, specifically in English, is mandated by the FAA for all levels of pilot certification. This requirement is rooted in the necessity for clear, unambiguous communication in the global aviation environment. English serves as the international language of aviation, facilitating interactions between pilots, air traffic controllers, and aviation professionals worldwide. Proficiency in English is therefore essential, not only for the safety of flight operations but also for the effective coordination within the complex network of global air traffic control. Candidates must demonstrate the ability to read, speak, write, and understand English to a level that ensures safe and effective communication during all phases of flight and ground operations.

These eligibility requirements—age and language proficiency—are designed to establish a baseline of maturity and communication ability for those entering the aviation field. They reflect the FAA's commitment to maintaining the highest standards of safety and operational integrity in the National Airspace System. By adhering to these criteria, the FAA ensures that individuals certified as pilots are equipped with the fundamental capabilities necessary to contribute positively to aviation safety and efficiency.

Medical Certificates

Medical certificates serve as a critical validation of an airman's physical and mental fitness to operate an aircraft safely within the National Airspace System. The Federal Aviation Administration (FAA) mandates that pilots and certain other airmen obtain and maintain an appropriate medical certificate to ensure they meet the stringent health and fitness standards required for the safe conduct of flight operations. The process of obtaining a medical certificate involves a thorough examination by an FAA-designated Aviation Medical Examiner (AME), who assesses the individual's health based on specific medical criteria set forth by the FAA.

The FAA classifies medical certificates into three distinct classes, each corresponding to the level of piloting privileges. First-Class Medical Certificates are required for Airline Transport Pilots, the highest level of pilot certification, reflecting the demanding health standards necessary for commercial airline operations. Second-Class Medical Certificates apply to commercial pilots engaged in non-airline duties, such as cargo transportation and charter operations. Third-Class Medical Certificates suffice for student, recreational, and private pilots, whose flying activities are generally considered less demanding than those of commercial pilots.

The examination for a medical certificate encompasses a comprehensive evaluation of the applicant's medical history, vision, hearing, equilibrium, mental health, and overall physical condition. Specific standards for vision include a requirement for distant vision of 20/20 or better in each eye, with or without correction, and the ability to perceive colors necessary for the safe performance of airman duties. Hearing tests ensure the applicant can hear an average conversational voice in a quiet room, using both ears, at a distance of six feet. The AME also evaluates the applicant's equilibrium to ensure no history or presence of conditions that could impair balance or spatial orientation, critical factors in the control of an aircraft.

Cardiovascular health is another area of focus, with the examination aiming to identify any history or symptoms of heart disease that could pose a risk during flight operations. The mental health assessment seeks to uncover any history of personality disorder, psychosis, bipolar disorder, or substance abuse that could impair judgment, reliability, or performance as a pilot. Applicants must disclose their entire medical history, including any previous surgeries, hospitalizations, and current medications, as part of the evaluation process.

Upon successful completion of the medical examination, the AME issues the medical certificate, which remains valid for a specific period depending on the class of certificate and the age of the airman. First-Class Medical Certificates are valid for 12 months for those under 40 years of age and 6 months for those 40 and older. Second-Class Medical Certificates have a validity of 12 months, while Third-Class Medical Certificates are valid for 60 months (5 years) for individuals under 40 and 24 months (2 years) for those 40 and older.

It is imperative for airmen to understand the conditions under which a medical certificate may be denied, suspended, or revoked. Conditions such as uncontrolled diabetes, epilepsy, certain cardiovascular diseases, and a history of substance abuse can lead to disqualification. However, the FAA does provide avenues for waivers or special issuances under certain circumstances, allowing individuals with disqualifying conditions to obtain a medical certificate provided they can demonstrate their condition is under control and does not adversely affect their ability to safely operate an aircraft.

Maintaining medical fitness is an ongoing responsibility for all certified airmen. Changes in health status, including new diagnoses, surgeries, or medications, must be reported to the FAA, and in some cases, may require a reevaluation of medical fitness. Airmen are encouraged to proactively manage their health and seek medical advice promptly for any conditions that could impact their flying privileges.

The medical certification process underscores the FAA's commitment to ensuring that the skies remain safe for all users of the National Airspace System. By adhering to these rigorous medical standards, airmen contribute to the overall safety and integrity of aviation operations, demonstrating their dedication to their own well-being and the safety of their passengers and fellow airmen.

The Certification Process

The certification process for aspiring aviators is a structured and comprehensive pathway that ensures candidates are thoroughly vetted for their knowledge, skills, and readiness to undertake the responsibilities of piloting aircraft within the National Airspace System. This process is meticulously designed by the Federal Aviation Administration (FAA) to uphold the highest standards of aviation safety and operational integrity, encompassing a series of regulatory prerequisites, examinations, and practical assessments that candidates must successfully navigate.

Initially, candidates must ensure they meet the foundational eligibility criteria, including age, language proficiency, and medical fitness, as previously detailed. Upon satisfying these initial requirements, the focus shifts to the acquisition of theoretical knowledge and practical flying skills pertinent to the specific certification sought. The FAA mandates completion of a prescribed amount of formal education and training, which can be obtained through FAA-approved flight schools or independent instructors certified under Title 14 of the Code of Federal Regulations (CFR) Part 61 or Part 141.

The theoretical component of the certification process involves rigorous study and understanding of a wide array of subjects relevant to aviation, including but not limited to aerodynamics, meteorology, FAA regulations, navigation, and aircraft operation and performance. Candidates are required to demonstrate their mastery of these subjects through written examinations, which are computer-based tests comprising multiple-choice questions. These exams are designed to evaluate the candidate's comprehension of critical aviation topics, ensuring a solid theoretical foundation for safe and effective piloting.

Following successful completion of the written exams, candidates must accumulate the requisite flight experience, specified in hours, which varies depending on the type of certification. This includes solo flights, cross-country navigation, night flying, and operations in various weather conditions, among others, providing a practical framework for applying theoretical knowledge in real-world flying scenarios. The accumulation of flight hours under the guidance of certified instructors allows candidates to develop and refine their flying skills, decision-making abilities, and situational awareness, all of which are crucial for safe aviation practices.

The culmination of the certification process is the practical test, commonly referred to as the check ride, which is administered by an FAA-designated pilot examiner. This comprehensive assessment evaluates the candidate's ability to safely and competently operate an aircraft in accordance with FAA standards. The check ride is divided into two segments: an oral examination, where candidates must demonstrate their theoretical knowledge and decision-making skills, and a flight test, during which they are required to perform a series of maneuvers and operational tasks. These tasks are outlined in the FAA's Practical Test Standards (PTS) or Airman Certification Standards (ACS), which detail the performance criteria for various flight maneuvers and operational procedures.

Successful completion of the practical test signifies that the candidate possesses the necessary competence, skill, and judgment to be certified as a pilot. Upon passing the check ride, the FAA issues the appropriate pilot certificate, marking the candidate's transition from student to certified pilot. It is imperative for newly certified pilots to continue honing their skills, expanding their knowledge, and adhering to FAA regulations and guidelines to ensure ongoing safety and proficiency in their aviation endeavors.

The certification process is a testament to the FAA's commitment to ensuring that individuals who earn pilot certifications are well-prepared to contribute positively to the aviation community and the safety of the National Airspace System. By adhering to this rigorous and structured process, candidates demonstrate their dedication to achieving the highest standards of aviation excellence, ready to embark on the challenging and rewarding journey of piloting aircraft.

Written Exams

Written exams serve as a pivotal step in the certification process for aspiring aviators, meticulously designed to evaluate a candidate's grasp of essential aviation knowledge, including FAA regulations, principles of flight, navigation, meteorology, and aircraft operations. These exams, administered by the Federal Aviation Administration (FAA), are computer-based and consist of multiple-choice questions, each crafted to assess the candidate's understanding and application of aviation theory and practice. The preparation for these exams demands a comprehensive study plan, encompassing a wide range of subjects pertinent to aviation safety and operations. Candidates are encouraged to utilize official FAA publications, such as the Pilot's Handbook of Aeronautical Knowledge and the Aeronautical Information Manual, as primary study materials. These resources provide invaluable insights into the intricacies of flight principles, air navigation, weather services, and airspace classification, among other topics.

In addition to FAA publications, aspiring pilots may benefit from supplementary study aids, including online courses, practice tests, and study guides specifically tailored to cover the breadth of knowledge required for the written exams. Engaging with a variety of study materials can enhance understanding and retention of complex concepts, facilitating a more thorough preparation for the exam. It is also advisable for candidates to participate in study groups or seek mentorship from certified flight instructors, as these interactions can offer new perspectives and clarify difficult topics.

The structure of the written exams reflects the diverse range of knowledge areas pertinent to pilot certification. Questions are formatted to challenge the candidate's ability to apply theoretical knowledge to practical scenarios, testing critical thinking and problem-solving skills in addition to factual recall. For instance, a question might present a weather scenario and ask the candidate to interpret how it could affect flight operations, requiring an understanding of weather patterns, aircraft performance, and FAA regulations.

To illustrate the nature of the questions encountered on the written exams, consider the following examples:

1. What is the primary purpose of the flaps on an aircraft?
[A] To increase the rate of climb
[B] To decrease landing distance
[C] To control the direction of flight
[D] To increase cruising speed

2. According to FAA regulations, what minimum visibility and cloud clearance are required for VFR flight in controlled airspace below 10,000 feet MSL?
[A] 1-mile visibility and clear of clouds
[B] 3-mile visibility and 500 feet below, 1,000 feet above, 2,000 feet horizontal distance from clouds

[C] 5-mile visibility and 1,000 feet below, 1,000 feet above, 1 mile horizontal distance from clouds
[D] 3-mile visibility and clear of clouds

3. When planning a cross-country flight, what factor should be considered when determining the fuel requirements?
[A] Wind direction and speed
[B] Type of aircraft
[C] Both A and B
[D] Neither A nor B

These questions exemplify the exam's focus on practical knowledge and decision-making, requiring candidates to draw upon their studies and apply information in a manner consistent with safe and efficient flight operations. Successful completion of the written exam is a testament to the candidate's readiness to proceed to the next stages of flight training and practical testing. It is a critical milestone in the certification process, affirming the candidate's foundational knowledge of aviation theory and practice.

Candidates are advised to approach the exam with a strategy that includes time management and an understanding of their own strengths and weaknesses. It is beneficial to answer questions confidently known first, marking more challenging questions for review if time permits. This approach ensures that candidates can secure as many accurate responses as possible, maximizing their score potential.

Upon passing the written exam, candidates receive an endorsement to proceed with the practical aspects of flight training, moving closer to achieving their goal of becoming certified pilots. The written exam, therefore, not only evaluates the candidate's knowledge but also serves as a bridge to the hands-on experience that is crucial for a successful aviation career.

Practical Tests

Question: What are the three main components evaluated during a practical test for pilot certification?

- A) Aircraft maintenance knowledge, weather prediction skills, and emergency procedure simulation.
- B) Pre-flight inspection procedures, in-flight maneuvers, and post-flight debriefing.
- C) Navigation planning, radio communication proficiency, and fuel management techniques.

Correct answer explanation: B) Pre-flight inspection procedures, in-flight maneuvers, and post-flight debriefing.

During a practical test, also known as a check ride, the examiner evaluates a candidate's ability to safely and competently perform a series of tasks. These tasks are designed to assess the candidate's practical knowledge and skills in three main areas:

1. **Pre-flight inspection procedures:** This component tests the candidate's ability to inspect the aircraft to ensure it is safe for flight. The candidate must demonstrate a thorough understanding of the aircraft's systems, the importance of checking for airworthiness directives, and the ability to identify any potential safety issues before taking off.

2. **In-flight maneuvers:** This section evaluates the candidate's ability to operate the aircraft under various conditions and perform specific maneuvers. These maneuvers may include takeoffs and landings, navigation using visual and instrument references, handling emergency situations, and adhering to air traffic control instructions. The candidate must show proficiency in managing the aircraft's controls and systems, applying correct procedures, and making sound decisions during flight.

3. **Post-flight debriefing:** After the flight, the examiner and the candidate discuss the flight to review performance. This debriefing is an essential component of the practical test as it provides an opportunity for the candidate to demonstrate their understanding of any errors made during the flight and how they would correct them in the future. It also allows the examiner to assess the candidate's ability to learn from their experiences and apply that knowledge to become a safer, more competent pilot.

These components ensure that the candidate possesses not only the technical knowledge and flying skills required but also the judgment and decision-making abilities essential for safe and effective piloting.

Chapter 4: Aircraft Maintenance and Repair

Annual inspections are a critical component of aircraft maintenance, mandated by the Federal Aviation Administration (FAA) to ensure that aircraft meet the stringent safety standards required for operation within the National Airspace System. These inspections are comprehensive evaluations of an aircraft's condition, including its systems, components, and overall airworthiness. The FAA requires that all aircraft, except those operating under special flight permits, undergo an annual inspection performed by a certified mechanic holding an Inspection Authorization (IA) from the FAA. The IA mechanic is specially qualified, having demonstrated a higher level of expertise and having met additional experience and testing requirements beyond those of a standard Airframe and Powerplant (A&P) mechanic.

The scope of the annual inspection is extensive, covering the aircraft from nose to tail and wingtip to wingtip. The inspection process includes, but is not limited to, examining the condition of the aircraft's structure, flight controls, landing gear, engine and propeller, fuel and exhaust systems, and avionics. Each component is meticulously checked for signs of wear, corrosion, damage, or any condition that could potentially compromise the safety of the aircraft. The inspection also involves testing the operation of the aircraft's systems and components to ensure they function correctly and within the manufacturer's specified tolerances.

One of the key aspects of the annual inspection is the adherence to the manufacturer's maintenance manuals and the FAA's regulations. The IA mechanic uses these documents as a guide to ensure that the inspection and any necessary repairs or adjustments are performed according to the established standards. Any discrepancies found during the inspection must be addressed and rectified before the aircraft can be deemed airworthy. In some cases, this may involve minor adjustments or repairs, while in others, it may require the replacement of parts or more significant repairs.

Upon completion of the annual inspection, the IA mechanic must make an entry in the aircraft's maintenance records, detailing the scope of the inspection, any discrepancies found, and the corrective actions taken. This record serves as a legal document attesting to the airworthiness of the aircraft at the time of the inspection. It is important for aircraft owners and operators to retain these records, as they provide a history of the aircraft's maintenance and are essential for ensuring continued compliance with FAA regulations.

The annual inspection is not only a regulatory requirement but also a critical practice for ensuring the safety and reliability of the aircraft. Regular inspections help to identify and address potential issues before they can lead to more serious problems or accidents. For aircraft owners and operators, staying informed about the requirements and procedures involved in the annual inspection process is essential. Understanding the importance of these inspections and ensuring they are conducted by qualified personnel are key steps in maintaining the safety, performance, and longevity of the aircraft.

In addition to the annual inspection, aircraft owners should also be aware of other maintenance requirements and inspections mandated by the FAA, such as 100-hour inspections for aircraft used for hire or flight instruction. These additional inspections further contribute to the overall safety and airworthiness of the aircraft, reinforcing the importance of a comprehensive and ongoing maintenance program. By adhering to these requirements and ensuring that their aircraft are regularly inspected and maintained, owners and operators play a crucial role in upholding the safety standards of the aviation industry.

Preventive Maintenance

Preventive maintenance stands as a cornerstone in ensuring the longevity, safety, and reliability of aircraft operations. This critical aspect of aircraft maintenance encompasses a range of activities designed to prevent problems before they occur, rather than addressing them after they have manifested. The Federal Aviation Administration (FAA) outlines specific preventive maintenance tasks that can be performed by certificated pilots, aside from those holding a sport pilot certificate, under Part 43 of the Federal Aviation Regulations (FAR). These tasks include, but are not limited to, oil changes, wheel bearing lubrication, hydraulic fluid replenishment, and the replacement of certain non-structural standard parts. It is imperative for aircraft owners and operators to familiarize themselves with these regulations to ensure compliance and maintain the airworthiness of their aircraft.

The execution of preventive maintenance requires meticulous attention to detail and adherence to the manufacturer's recommended maintenance schedules. These schedules are crafted based on extensive testing and operational experience, aiming to identify and mitigate potential failures before they pose a risk to flight safety. For instance, the timely replacement of wear-and-tear parts like spark plugs, belts, and hoses can prevent unexpected engine failures during flight. Similarly, regular inspection and servicing of the aircraft's electrical systems can preempt electrical failures that could lead to loss of instrumentation or lighting.

Moreover, preventive maintenance is not solely limited to the mechanical aspects of the aircraft. It also includes the calibration of avionics equipment, inspection of emergency equipment, and verification of software updates for onboard systems. These actions are critical in ensuring that all components of the aircraft function cohesively and reliably, particularly under adverse conditions.

For aircraft operators, engaging in preventive maintenance also has economic benefits. By proactively addressing maintenance needs, operators can avoid the higher costs associated with unscheduled repairs, which often require expedited shipping of parts and can result in significant downtime for the aircraft. Furthermore, a well-maintained aircraft retains a higher resale value and ensures greater operational availability.

To facilitate effective preventive maintenance, aircraft maintenance records play a pivotal role. These records provide a detailed history of all maintenance activities performed on the aircraft, including the date of service, description of the work completed, and identification of the personnel involved. This documentation is essential for tracking the maintenance status of the aircraft, planning future maintenance activities, and demonstrating compliance with regulatory requirements.

In summary, preventive maintenance is an indispensable practice within the realm of aircraft operations, embodying a proactive approach to maintenance that prioritizes safety, reliability, and cost-effectiveness. By adhering to established maintenance schedules, leveraging detailed maintenance records, and complying with FAA regulations, aircraft owners and operators can ensure that their aircraft remain airworthy and perform optimally over their operational lifespan.

Required Inspections

The Federal Aviation Administration mandates a series of required inspections to ensure the continued airworthiness and safety of aircraft. These inspections are critical components of a comprehensive maintenance program, designed to identify and rectify potential issues before they compromise safety. Among these, the most notable are the Annual and 100-Hour inspections, each serving a distinct purpose yet equally vital in maintaining the operational integrity of aircraft.

The Annual Inspection, as its name suggests, is required once every 12 months for all aircraft. This exhaustive examination covers the entire aircraft, including its systems, components, and avionics, ensuring that everything functions correctly and adheres to the safety standards set forth by the FAA. Only an FAA-certified Airframe and Powerplant (A&P) mechanic with an Inspection Authorization (IA) can conduct this inspection. The meticulous nature of the Annual Inspection necessitates a thorough review of the aircraft's logbooks, maintenance records, and adherence to all applicable airworthiness directives.

Simultaneously, the 100-Hour Inspection is specifically mandated for aircraft that are used for hire or flight instruction. Like the Annual Inspection, it encompasses a comprehensive check of the aircraft's systems and components. However, its frequency is determined by the aircraft's operational hours, requiring completion every 100 hours of flight time. This inspection is crucial for aircraft engaged in commercial operations, ensuring they remain safe for both instructors and students. Although the 100-Hour Inspection does not necessitate an IA-certified mechanic, it must be performed by an A&P mechanic or an FAA-certified repair station.

Both inspections follow a detailed checklist provided in the aircraft's maintenance manual, a document tailored to the specific make and model by the manufacturer. This checklist ensures no component is overlooked, from the fuselage and flight controls to the engine and onboard electronics. The process involves both visual inspections and functional tests, with any identified issues requiring immediate rectification to meet the FAA's stringent airworthiness criteria.

In addition to these primary inspections, aircraft owners and operators must also be cognizant of other required checks and maintenance routines. These include Airworthiness Directives (ADs) issued by the FAA to address safety issues discovered in specific aircraft models or components. Compliance with ADs is mandatory and time-sensitive, with the aim of mitigating potential hazards. Similarly, Service Bulletins (SBs) issued by manufacturers, though not always mandatory, provide important information on recommended maintenance practices and modifications to enhance safety and performance.

The importance of adhering to these required inspections cannot be overstated. They are foundational to flight safety, ensuring that every aircraft meets the FAA's rigorous standards for operation. By diligently following the inspection schedules and maintenance requirements, aircraft owners and operators not only comply with regulatory mandates but also contribute to the overarching goal of aviation safety. Through this commitment to maintenance and inspection, the aviation community continues to uphold the highest standards of safety and reliability in air travel.

Annual Inspections

Question: What is the primary purpose of an annual inspection, and who is authorized to perform it?

- A) To assess the aircraft's cosmetic condition, performed by any licensed pilot.
- B) To ensure the aircraft meets safety and operational standards, performed by an FAA-certified mechanic with an Inspection Authorization (IA).
- C) To update the aircraft's avionics systems, performed by the manufacturer.

Correct answer explanation: B) To ensure the aircraft meets safety and operational standards, performed by an FAA-certified mechanic with an Inspection Authorization (IA).

The primary purpose of an annual inspection is to verify that the aircraft complies with all safety and operational standards as mandated by the Federal Aviation Administration (FAA). This comprehensive inspection covers various aspects of the aircraft, including its structural integrity, engine and system functions, and compliance with airworthiness directives. Only an FAA-certified mechanic who has been granted an Inspection Authorization (IA) is qualified to conduct this inspection. The IA mechanic has demonstrated a higher level of expertise and has been given the authority by the FAA to perform these critical inspections, ensuring that the aircraft is safe for operation. This process is essential for maintaining the safety and reliability of the aircraft, and it must be completed annually for the aircraft to be legally operated under the regulations set forth by the FAA.

100-Hour Inspections

The 100-Hour Inspection, mandated for aircraft utilized in instruction or for hire, plays a pivotal role in ensuring the safety and airworthiness of these frequently used aircraft. This inspection is comprehensive, scrutinizing the aircraft's systems, components, and overall condition to identify any potential issues that could compromise safety. Unlike the Annual Inspection, which requires an FAA-certified Airframe and Powerplant (A&P) mechanic with an Inspection Authorization (IA), the 100-Hour Inspection can be performed by any qualified A&P mechanic or an FAA-certified repair station, making it more accessible for operators to maintain compliance.

During the 100-Hour Inspection, mechanics follow a manufacturer-provided checklist specific to the aircraft's make and model. This checklist is the cornerstone of the inspection, ensuring a systematic review of critical areas such as the engine, propeller, flight controls, landing gear, and onboard electronics. Each item on the checklist must be inspected, tested, or measured to verify its condition and functionality meets the FAA's stringent standards. If any discrepancies or issues are found, they must be addressed and rectified before the aircraft can be deemed airworthy and returned to service.

This inspection not only ensures the mechanical integrity of the aircraft but also serves as a preventive measure against wear and tear that could lead to more significant problems down the line. By identifying and fixing minor issues early, the 100-Hour Inspection contributes to the longevity of the aircraft and enhances safety for both instructors and students. Additionally, maintaining a rigorous inspection schedule supports the overall reliability of the aircraft, reducing the likelihood of unscheduled maintenance and downtime.

Compliance with the 100-Hour Inspection requirement is not just a regulatory mandate but a critical component of responsible aircraft operation. It underscores the commitment of aircraft operators to uphold the highest safety standards, ensuring that every flight conducted under their purview adheres to the FAA's operational safety criteria. Through diligent adherence to these inspection schedules, the aviation community continues to foster a culture of safety and excellence in aviation operations.

Maintenance Records

Maintenance records serve as a critical component of the aircraft's documentation, providing a comprehensive log of all maintenance, repair, and alteration activities performed. These records are not merely administrative tools but are fundamental to ensuring the ongoing airworthiness and safety of the aircraft. The Federal Aviation Administration (FAA) mandates the meticulous recording and retention of these records to facilitate oversight, compliance checks, and to support the investigative process in the event of an incident or accident. Each entry in the maintenance records must include specific information such as the date of the maintenance activity, a description of the work performed, the name of the person who carried out the maintenance along with their signature, and, if applicable, their certificate number. This level of detail ensures transparency and accountability in aircraft maintenance operations.

The structure and organization of maintenance records can vary, but they typically encompass the aircraft's logbooks, which include the airframe, engine, and propeller logbooks, along with additional records for any major alterations or repairs. The airframe logbook documents all work done on the aircraft's structure, control systems, and interior components. The engine and propeller logbooks, respectively, keep track of maintenance performed on these critical components, including routine inspections, overhauls, repairs, and replacements. Records of major alterations or repairs provide a history of significant changes to the aircraft's configuration or structure, which is essential for understanding its current state and for planning future maintenance activities.

It's imperative for aircraft owners and operators to understand the regulatory requirements surrounding the retention of maintenance records. The FAA requires that certain records be kept for the life of the aircraft, such as records of major alterations, while others, like routine maintenance and repair records, may have specified retention periods. Failure to properly maintain and retain these records can lead to regulatory non-compliance and can significantly impact the aircraft's resale value, as potential buyers or leasing companies will scrutinize these records to assess the aircraft's condition and maintenance history.

In addition to regulatory compliance, well-organized and complete maintenance records play a pivotal role in maintaining operational efficiency and safety. They enable maintenance personnel to track the aircraft's maintenance history, identify recurring issues, and plan for upcoming maintenance activities. This proactive approach to maintenance can prevent minor issues from escalating into major problems, thereby enhancing the safety and reliability of the aircraft. Furthermore, comprehensive maintenance records can expedite the troubleshooting process, saving valuable time and resources.

For operators looking to digitize their maintenance records, several software solutions offer robust record-keeping capabilities. These digital platforms can simplify the management of maintenance records, improve accessibility, and provide enhanced tracking and reporting features. However, it's crucial to ensure that any digital record-keeping system complies with FAA regulations regarding the format, accessibility, and security of electronic maintenance records.

In conclusion, the diligent management of maintenance records is a cornerstone of responsible aircraft operation. These records not only ensure compliance with regulatory requirements but also contribute significantly to the safety, reliability, and value of the aircraft. By prioritizing accurate and thorough record-keeping, aircraft owners and operators can safeguard their investment and uphold the highest standards of airworthiness and safety.

Chapter 5: Aeronautical Information Manual

The Aeronautical Information Manual (AIM) serves as a comprehensive guide designed to provide aviators with detailed information on operating within the National Airspace System (NAS) of the United States. It encompasses a wide array of topics crucial for pilots, including but not limited to, the fundamentals of airspace, procedures for communication with Air Traffic Control (ATC), weather services, navigation, and emergency procedures. The AIM is structured to assist pilots in understanding the complex environment in which they operate, ensuring that they can perform their duties with an enhanced level of safety and efficiency. This manual is not only a resource for seasoned aviators but also serves as an essential tool for students and instructors, offering a foundation upon which pilots can build their knowledge and skills.

The AIM's section on airspace classification is particularly noteworthy, providing pilots with a clear understanding of the different types of airspace that exist within the NAS and the specific operating rules and requirements for each. This includes detailed descriptions of Class A, B, C, D, E, and G airspaces, each with its unique characteristics and regulations. For example, Class B airspace is designed to protect and manage the busy airspace surrounding the nation's largest airports, requiring pilots to obtain ATC clearance before entry. In contrast, Class G airspace, often found in rural or less populated areas, does not require such clearance, reflecting its more open and accessible nature.

Navigation aids and services are another critical component covered in the AIM, offering insights into the various systems available to assist pilots in navigating the skies. This includes traditional radio navigation aids like VORs (VHF Omnidirectional Range) and NDBs (Non-Directional Beacons), as well as modern GPS (Global Positioning System) technology. The manual provides practical information on how these aids work, how pilots can use them effectively, and the limitations of each system. Understanding these navigation aids is essential for both VFR (Visual Flight Rules) and IFR (Instrument Flight Rules) operations, ensuring pilots can maintain their intended flight path and reach their destinations safely.

Emergency procedures constitute another pivotal section within the AIM, outlining the steps pilots should take in various unexpected situations. This ranges from engine failures and in-flight fires to urgent medical situations and forced landings. The AIM emphasizes the importance of remaining calm, maintaining control of the aircraft, and following established procedures to manage the emergency effectively. These guidelines are designed to prepare pilots for the rare but critical moments when quick, decisive action is necessary to ensure the safety of both crew and passengers.

In addition to these topics, the AIM also addresses the importance of effective communication with ATC, providing protocols for radio communication that facilitate clear, concise exchanges between pilots and controllers. This includes standard phraseology, proper use of radio equipment, and procedures for communicating in both routine and emergency situations. Effective communication is a cornerstone of aviation safety, reducing the risk of misunderstandings and ensuring that pilots and ATC can work together smoothly to manage the flow of air traffic.

The AIM is updated regularly to reflect changes in regulations, procedures, and technology, ensuring that it remains a current and relevant resource for the aviation community. Pilots are encouraged to familiarize themselves with the latest edition of the AIM and to incorporate its guidance into their daily operations. By doing so, they contribute to the overall safety and efficiency of the NAS, demonstrating their commitment to professionalism and their dedication to upholding the highest standards of aviation practice.

Airspace Classification

Airspace classification in the United States is delineated into several categories, each with distinct rules and requirements designed to ensure the safety and efficiency of air navigation. The classifications include Class A, B, C, D, E, and G airspaces. Class A airspace encompasses altitudes from 18,000 feet mean sea level (MSL) up to and including flight level 600 (approximately 60,000 feet MSL). Operations within Class A airspace require pilots to operate their aircraft under Instrument Flight Rules (IFR), and an air traffic control (ATC) clearance is mandatory for entry. This airspace is primarily designed for overflight or high-altitude, cross-country flights and is not typically encountered by general aviation pilots on a regular basis.

Class B airspace is structured around the nation's busiest airports to manage the high volume of air traffic with enhanced safety measures. It extends from the surface to a specified upper limit, often shaped like an inverted wedding cake to accommodate the varied needs of arriving and departing aircraft. Pilots must obtain an ATC clearance before entering Class B airspace and are required to have a Mode C transponder. The primary goal within Class B airspace is to prevent mid-air collisions, especially during peak operational hours, by maintaining strict separation between all aircraft.

Class C airspace is designed for airports with a moderate level of air traffic. Similar to Class B, it features a procedural airspace configuration that typically consists of a 5-nautical mile radius core surface area up to 4,000 feet above the airport elevation, surrounded by a 10-nautical mile radius shelf area that extends from 1,200 feet to 4,000 feet above the airport elevation. Pilots must establish two-way radio communication with ATC before entering Class C airspace, and a Mode C transponder is required.

Class D airspace is found around airports with operational control towers but generally less air traffic volume than those warranting Class B or C designations. The airspace extends from the surface up to 2,500 feet above the airport elevation and usually has a radius of 4 to 5 nautical miles. Two-way radio communication must be established with the control tower before entering, and while a Mode C transponder is not a requirement, it is recommended for enhanced situational awareness.

Class E airspace is the most common type of controlled airspace and includes all controlled airspace not designated as Class A, B, C, or D. It is designed to accommodate controlled flights under Instrument Flight Rules (IFR) as well as to provide controlled airspace for Visual Flight Rules (VFR) flights. Class E airspace begins at either the surface, 700 feet AGL, or 1,200 feet AGL, extending upward to, but not including, 18,000 feet MSL, unless designated otherwise. No specific ATC clearance is required for VFR flights to enter Class E airspace, but pilots are expected to adhere to the applicable operational requirements.

Class G airspace is uncontrolled and extends from the surface to the base of the overlying Class E airspace. It is the only airspace where neither IFR nor VFR flights require ATC clearance or communication. However, pilots are encouraged to remain vigilant and maintain clear communication with nearby aircraft to ensure safety. Operating in Class G airspace offers pilots the most freedom but also demands a high level of responsibility and situational awareness to avoid conflicts with other airspace users.

Understanding the distinctions between these airspace classifications is crucial for pilots to navigate the National Airspace System safely and efficiently. Each class of airspace is designed with specific operational requirements to manage the mix of aircraft types and volumes of traffic, ensuring that safety protocols are maintained. Pilots must familiarize themselves with the characteristics and requirements of each airspace classification and plan their flights accordingly, taking into consideration the need for ATC clearances, communication procedures, and equipment requirements to comply with the regulations governing the airspace through which they intend to fly.

Controlled Airspace

Controlled airspace is designated to facilitate a safe and efficient environment for aircraft operations, particularly where high volumes of air traffic are present. This airspace is governed by specific rules and regulations that pilots must adhere to, including entry, communication, and equipment requirements. The classification of controlled airspace into Classes A, B, C, D, and E, each with its unique operational requirements, underscores the Federal Aviation Administration's (FAA) commitment to maintaining the highest standards of air safety and navigation efficiency.

Class A airspace, for instance, requires all aircraft to be equipped with an operable Mode C transponder and to adhere strictly to Instrument Flight Rules (IFR). This high-altitude airspace, starting at 18,000 feet mean sea level (MSL) up to and including flight level 600, is predominantly used for overflight or long-distance, cross-country flights by aircraft capable of high-altitude operations. The mandatory use of IFR in Class A airspace ensures that all aircraft are under the control of air traffic control (ATC), thus significantly reducing the risk of mid-air collisions.

In contrast, Class B airspace is designed to protect the airspace surrounding the nation's busiest airports. The structure of Class B airspace, often described as an inverted wedding cake, provides a controlled environment for a diverse mix of aircraft operations, from commercial airliners to private general aviation flights. Entry into Class B airspace requires explicit ATC clearance, and all aircraft must be equipped with a Mode C transponder. The stringent requirements for operating in Class B airspace, including pilot certification and aircraft equipment standards, are reflective of the FAA's prioritization of safety in areas of intense air traffic.

Class C and D airspaces cater to airports with varying levels of air traffic, with Class C surrounding airports with a moderate level of air traffic and Class D for those with operational control towers but generally less traffic volume. Both classifications require pilots to establish two-way radio communication with ATC before entry, but only Class C mandates the use of a Mode C transponder. These airspaces are tailored to ensure that aircraft can operate safely in proximity to airports, with Class C providing a higher level of control to manage the mix of commercial, cargo, and general aviation flights.

Class E airspace, the most common type of controlled airspace, encompasses all controlled airspace not classified as Class A, B, C, or D. It serves as a regulatory framework for both IFR and Visual Flight Rules (VFR) operations, facilitating a safe transition between different airspaces and supporting the efficient management of air traffic. Unlike the other classes, Class E does not have specific entry requirements for VFR flights, but pilots are expected to comply with the operational requirements applicable to this airspace.

The delineation and regulation of controlled airspace are essential components of the National Airspace System, ensuring that the diverse needs of all airspace users are met while maintaining the highest levels of safety. Pilots must possess a thorough understanding of the characteristics and requirements of each airspace classification to navigate the skies safely and efficiently. This includes knowledge of the altitudes and boundaries of the airspace, the necessary ATC clearances, and the equipment and communication protocols required for operation within these controlled environments. By adhering to the regulations governing controlled airspace, pilots contribute to the overall safety and operational efficiency of the aviation community, ensuring that the skies remain safe for all users.

Uncontrolled Airspace

Uncontrolled airspace, designated as Class G airspace, is the segment of the National Airspace System where the Federal Aviation Administration (FAA) does not provide air traffic control services to aircraft operating within this airspace under Visual Flight Rules (VFR). This type of airspace extends from the surface to the base of the overlying Class E airspace, varying in altitude depending on geographical location and the presence of controlled airspace above it. Within Class G airspace, pilots are afforded the most freedom regarding flight operations, yet they bear the full responsibility for collision avoidance, navigation, and determining weather minimums suitable for safe flight.

Operating in Class G airspace does not necessitate communication with Air Traffic Control (ATC), nor is there a requirement for an aircraft to be equipped with a transponder. However, it is imperative for pilots to exercise vigilance and adhere to the see-and-avoid principle, a fundamental aspect of VFR flight. This principle underscores the pilot's responsibility to remain constantly alert and visually scan the airspace for other aircraft, particularly during takeoff, landing, and when flying at lower altitudes where Class G airspace is most commonly encountered.

The regulations governing VFR flight in Class G airspace are designed to ensure that pilots maintain adequate visibility and cloud clearance, which vary according to the time of day and altitude. During the day at less than 1,200 feet above ground level (AGL), pilots must maintain clear of clouds with at least 1 statute mile (SM) of visibility. For flights above 1,200 feet AGL but below 10,000 feet mean sea level (MSL), the visibility requirement increases to 1 SM, and aircraft must remain at least 500 feet below, 1,000 feet above, or 2,000 feet horizontally from any cloud. At night, the visibility requirement for all altitudes in Class G airspace up to 10,000 feet MSL is 3 SM, with the same cloud clearance requirements as daytime operations.

Pilots navigating through Class G airspace must be proficient in reading aeronautical charts to accurately identify the boundaries of this uncontrolled airspace and the transition to controlled airspace, where different rules and requirements apply. It is also essential for pilots to be familiar with the operational limitations of their aircraft and personal limitations, especially when operating in Class G airspace, where self-reliance is paramount. Weather conditions can change rapidly, and without the guidance of ATC, pilots must be prepared to make independent decisions to ensure flight safety.

Flight planning for operations in Class G airspace should include a thorough pre-flight weather briefing, even though ATC services are not utilized. This briefing will provide valuable information on weather conditions, temporary flight restrictions (TFRs), and Notices to Airmen (NOTAMs) that could affect the flight. Additionally, pilots are encouraged to use available navigation aids and technology, such as GPS, to enhance situational awareness and navigation precision during flight.

While Class G airspace offers the most freedom for VFR flight, it also demands a high level of airmanship, situational awareness, and decision-making skills from pilots. The absence of ATC services does not diminish the importance of adhering to VFR flight rules and regulations designed to maintain the safety of all airspace users. Pilots operating in Class G airspace contribute to the overall safety of the aviation community by exercising good judgment, maintaining proficiency in VFR navigation and communication procedures, and by always being prepared for the unexpected.

Navigation Aids and Services

Navigation aids and services play a crucial role in the safety and efficiency of air travel, providing pilots with the necessary information to navigate the skies accurately. These aids range from ground-based technologies to satellite systems, each designed to assist in the precise determination of an aircraft's position and direction. Among the most widely recognized navigation aids are the VHF Omnidirectional Range (VOR), the Global Positioning System (GPS), and the Instrument Landing System (ILS).

The VHF Omnidirectional Range system, or VOR, is a type of short-range radio navigation system that enables aircraft with a receiving unit to determine their position and stay on course by receiving radio signals transmitted by a network of fixed ground radio beacons. It offers high levels of accuracy and reliability, which is why it has been a staple in aviation navigation for decades. Pilots use VOR by tuning into the VOR station frequency and interpreting the signals received to ascertain their bearing relative to the station, thus facilitating route navigation and intersection holding.

The Global Positioning System, known as GPS, represents a significant advancement in navigation technology, utilizing a constellation of satellites orbiting the Earth to provide geolocation and time information to a GPS receiver anywhere on or near the Earth where there is an unobstructed line of sight to four or more GPS satellites. This system is invaluable for pilots for its ability to offer real-time position information with remarkable accuracy, which is essential for route planning, en route navigation, and approaches. The widespread adoption of GPS has enhanced the safety and efficiency of flight operations, allowing for more direct routes and reducing the reliance on ground-based navigation aids.

The Instrument Landing System, or ILS, is a precision approach system that provides guidance to aircraft approaching a runway to ensure a safe landing, especially under conditions of reduced visibility. It consists of two main components: the localizer, which provides lateral guidance; and the glide slope, which provides vertical guidance. Together, these components guide the aircraft down to the runway threshold. ILS is critical for operations in adverse weather conditions, enabling pilots to conduct approaches and landings when visual references are minimal.

In addition to these primary navigation aids, there are other systems and services designed to support navigation in various phases of flight. These include the Automatic Dependent Surveillance-Broadcast (ADS-B), which allows aircraft to broadcast their position to other aircraft and air traffic control, and the Distance Measuring Equipment (DME), which measures the slant range distance between an aircraft and a ground station. Both systems enhance situational awareness and contribute to the safety of flight operations.

Pilots must be proficient in using these navigation aids and services, understanding their operational principles, limitations, and the procedures for their use. This knowledge is critical for planning flights, executing navigation tasks, and making informed decisions in response to changing conditions or in the event of system failures. Training and continuous learning are essential for pilots to maintain competency in navigation, ensuring that they can leverage these aids and services effectively to conduct safe and efficient flight operations.

Emergency Procedures

Emergency procedures are a critical component of aviation safety, ensuring that pilots and crew are prepared to handle unexpected situations effectively. These procedures encompass a wide range of scenarios, including engine failures, in-flight fires, electrical failures, and medical emergencies among others. Each type of emergency requires a specific set of actions to be taken, often under time-sensitive conditions, to mitigate risks and ensure the safety of all onboard.

For engine failures, the immediate priority is to maintain aircraft control while identifying a suitable area for an emergency landing. Pilots are trained to follow a specific engine-out procedure, which includes maintaining optimal glide speed, executing a mayday call if possible, and preparing the aircraft and passengers for an off-airport landing. The effectiveness of handling such emergencies relies heavily on the pilot's ability to remain calm, make rapid decisions, and execute the necessary maneuvers with precision.

In the event of an in-flight fire, the primary goal is to identify the source of the fire, isolate it if possible, and extinguish it. Electrical fires may require shutting down the aircraft's electrical system, while cabin fires might necessitate the use of fire extinguishers and ensuring that smoke does not overwhelm the cabin by using oxygen masks if available. Training emphasizes the importance of quick detection and response to prevent the fire from spreading and to minimize the inhalation of toxic fumes.

Electrical failures present unique challenges, particularly at night or in instrument meteorological conditions, where the loss of navigational and communication equipment can severely impact the pilot's ability to maintain situational awareness. Pilots are taught to rely on basic flight instruments and to follow emergency procedures that prioritize maintaining control of the aircraft, finding alternate means of navigation, and establishing communication with air traffic control using backup systems if available.

Medical emergencies require a different approach, focusing on providing immediate care to the affected individual while ensuring the continued safe operation of the aircraft. This may involve administering first aid, using onboard medical kits, and potentially diverting the flight to the nearest suitable airport where medical assistance is available. Crew members receive training in basic first aid and are familiarized with the medical resources available on the aircraft to address such situations effectively.

Each of these emergency scenarios is addressed in the Aeronautical Information Manual with detailed procedures and recommended practices. Pilots are encouraged to familiarize themselves thoroughly with these procedures, to participate in regular training and simulation exercises, and to maintain a level of preparedness that enables them to respond decisively and effectively in the event of an emergency. The manual also emphasizes the importance of pre-flight planning, regular maintenance checks, and adherence to safety protocols as proactive measures to minimize the risk of emergencies. Through comprehensive preparation and ongoing education, pilots can enhance the safety and security of flight operations, ensuring that they are well-equipped to manage the challenges that may arise during flight.

Chapter 6: Air Traffic Control (ATC)

Air Traffic Control (ATC) services and communications are pivotal for the safety and efficiency of all flight operations, encompassing a broad spectrum of activities that facilitate the smooth flow of air traffic within the global airspace system. ATC responsibilities include traffic management, providing navigational assistance, and ensuring that aircraft maintain safe distances from each other. This is achieved through a structured communication protocol that pilots and air traffic controllers adhere to, ensuring clarity and preventing misunderstandings that could lead to safety incidents.

The ATC system is divided into various sectors, each managed by a specific type of air traffic control facility. These include the Air Route Traffic Control Centers (ARTCCs) responsible for managing high-altitude flights across large regions, Terminal Radar Approach Control (TRACON) facilities that handle aircraft approaching and departing busy airports, and Air Traffic Control Towers (ATCT) that manage the immediate airspace surrounding an airport and aircraft ground movements. Each of these facilities plays a crucial role in managing the complex flow of air traffic, utilizing radar and communication systems to monitor and direct aircraft.

Communication between pilots and air traffic controllers is conducted primarily through radio transmissions using very high frequency (VHF) bands. Pilots are required to maintain constant communication with ATC when flying in controlled airspace, receiving clearances, instructions, and information that assist in navigation and collision avoidance. Standardized phraseology is used to minimize the risk of miscommunication, with specific terms and procedures outlined in the Pilot/Controller Glossary. This standardized language ensures that pilots and controllers, regardless of their native language, can communicate effectively.

Pilots initiate contact with ATC by providing their aircraft identification, location, altitude, and intentions. Controllers respond with instructions for course adjustments, altitude changes, or speed modifications as necessary to maintain safe separation from other aircraft and to expedite the flow of air traffic. In addition to voice communications, modern ATC systems also utilize digital data communication methods, such as the Automatic Dependent Surveillance-Broadcast (ADS-B) system, which automatically transmits the precise location of an aircraft to ATC and other nearby aircraft equipped with ADS-B receivers. This technology enhances situational awareness and allows for more efficient routing and spacing of aircraft.

Radar services are another critical component of ATC, enabling controllers to track the position, speed, and altitude of aircraft within their sector. Primary radar systems detect aircraft by bouncing radio waves off their surfaces, while secondary radar systems receive transponder signals from aircraft, providing more detailed information about the aircraft's identity and altitude. This radar coverage is essential for maintaining safe separation between aircraft, particularly in areas of high traffic density or when visibility is poor.

ATC also plays a vital role in emergency situations, providing guidance and support to pilots in distress. Controllers can coordinate search and rescue operations, reroute other aircraft to clear airspace for emergency landings, and provide critical information to pilots, such as nearest airports, weather conditions, and terrain information. The ability of ATC to respond quickly and effectively in emergencies is a testament to the training and professionalism of air traffic controllers, who are trained to maintain composure under pressure and to make rapid decisions to ensure the safety of all aircraft under their control.

In summary, ATC services and communications are fundamental to the operation of the global airspace system, ensuring that air traffic flows smoothly and safely. Through a combination of sophisticated technology, standardized communication protocols, and the expertise of air traffic controllers, the ATC system manages the complex interactions between thousands of aircraft in the sky at any given time, demonstrating the remarkable efficiency and safety of modern air travel.

ATC Services and Communications

Air Traffic Control (ATC) services and communications play a critical role in the orchestration of the airspace, ensuring the safety and efficiency of flights by managing the complex dynamics of air traffic. The foundation of these services rests on the principles of traffic management, navigational assistance, and the enforcement of regulations designed to maintain safe distances between aircraft. Through a structured protocol of communication, ATC and pilots engage in a continuous exchange of information, utilizing a standardized phraseology that is critical for the clarity and precision required in aviation operations.

The ATC infrastructure is segmented into various sectors, each overseen by specialized facilities including Air Route Traffic Control Centers (ARTCCs), Terminal Radar Approach Control (TRACON) facilities, and Air Traffic Control Towers (ATCT). ARTCCs are pivotal in managing extensive regions of airspace, particularly focusing on high-altitude, en-route flight operations. TRACON facilities provide crucial services for aircraft in the approach and departure phases near airports, while ATCTs are responsible for the immediate airspace surrounding airports, including takeoffs, landings, and ground movements. This structured division ensures a seamless flow of air traffic, with each facility equipped with sophisticated radar and communication systems to monitor and guide aircraft effectively.

Communication between pilots and air traffic controllers is predominantly conducted via radio transmissions within the very high frequency (VHF) bands. This constant communication is imperative in controlled airspace, where pilots receive instructions, clearances, and vital information to aid in navigation and collision avoidance. The use of standardized phraseology, as outlined in the Pilot/Controller Glossary, minimizes the risk of miscommunication. This common language, irrespective of the native language of the pilots or controllers, is essential for effective communication.

Upon initiating contact with ATC, pilots provide their aircraft identification, location, altitude, and intentions, to which controllers respond with specific instructions to ensure the safe and orderly flow of air traffic. These instructions may include course adjustments, altitude changes, or modifications to airspeed. The integration of digital data communication methods, such as the Automatic Dependent Surveillance-Broadcast (ADS-B) system, complements voice communications by automatically transmitting precise location data of aircraft to ATC and other equipped aircraft, enhancing situational awareness and operational efficiency.

Radar services constitute a fundamental aspect of ATC, enabling the tracking of aircraft positions, velocities, and altitudes. The synergy of primary and secondary radar systems provides a comprehensive overview of the airspace, with primary radars detecting aircraft by reflecting radio waves and secondary radars receiving transponder signals that offer detailed aircraft information. This radar coverage is indispensable for maintaining safe separation between aircraft, especially under conditions of high traffic density or reduced visibility.

In emergency situations, the role of ATC is magnified as they provide pivotal guidance and support to pilots in distress. The capability of ATC to swiftly coordinate search and rescue operations, reroute traffic to facilitate emergency landings, and furnish pilots with critical information underscores the importance of ATC services in ensuring the safety and security of flight operations. The professionalism and training of air traffic controllers equip them to handle high-pressure situations effectively, making rapid decisions to safeguard all aircraft under their jurisdiction.

The intricate network of ATC services and communications underscores the complexity and efficiency of modern air travel. By managing the interactions between thousands of aircraft simultaneously in the sky, ATC services demonstrate the remarkable capabilities of the global airspace system, ensuring that air traffic flows smoothly and safely. Through the combination of advanced technology, standardized communication practices, and the expertise of air traffic controllers, the ATC system plays an indispensable role in the aviation industry, facilitating the safe and efficient movement of aircraft around the world.

Radar Services

Radar services, provided by Air Traffic Control (ATC), are essential for the surveillance and management of aircraft within controlled airspace. These services utilize advanced radar systems to continuously monitor the speed, direction, and altitude of aircraft, ensuring safe separation between flights and efficient navigation through congested airspaces. The primary function of radar services is to augment the safety and efficiency of air navigation by providing real-time data to air traffic controllers, enabling them to make informed decisions and issue precise instructions to pilots.

The radar system employed by ATC can be categorized into two main types: primary and secondary radar. Primary radar works by emitting radio waves that bounce off objects, such as aircraft, and return to the radar antenna. This type of radar provides information on the location and distance of an aircraft from the radar site but does not identify the aircraft. Secondary radar, on the other hand, relies on a transponder in the aircraft that responds to signals sent by the radar. This response includes specific information about the aircraft, such as its identification, altitude, and speed, offering a more comprehensive picture of the airspace situation.

One of the key advantages of radar services is the ability to track aircraft in areas where visual observation is not possible, such as at night or in poor weather conditions. This capability is critical for maintaining continuous surveillance of all aircraft within a controller's assigned airspace, ensuring that safe distances are kept between aircraft and that potential conflicts are identified and resolved promptly.

Radar services also play a pivotal role in managing air traffic flow, particularly during peak travel times or in the vicinity of major airports. By providing accurate, real-time data on aircraft positions and velocities, controllers can optimize flight paths, reduce the need for in-flight holding patterns, and minimize delays. This level of control is vital for maintaining the efficiency of the national airspace system and ensuring that flights arrive and depart as scheduled.

In addition to traffic management and surveillance, radar services are instrumental in assisting with navigation and providing support during emergencies. For aircraft experiencing navigational equipment failures or in distress, radar services can offer precise guidance and coordinate with search and rescue operations to ensure the safety of passengers and crew.

The integration of radar data with other technologies, such as Automatic Dependent Surveillance-Broadcast (ADS-B) and Traffic Collision Avoidance Systems (TCAS), further enhances the safety and efficiency of flight operations. ADS-B, for example, allows aircraft to broadcast their position and velocity to ATC and other nearby aircraft equipped with ADS-B receivers, providing an additional layer of situational awareness. TCAS, meanwhile, uses radar and transponder signals to detect potential collision threats and advise pilots on avoidance maneuvers.

Despite the sophistication of radar and associated technologies, the human element remains crucial. Air traffic controllers are extensively trained to interpret radar displays, understand the capabilities and limitations of radar systems, and apply this knowledge to manage air traffic safely and efficiently. Their expertise enables them to quickly identify and address potential issues, guiding pilots through complex airspace with precision and care.

Radar services, therefore, are a cornerstone of modern air traffic control, combining advanced technology with professional expertise to safeguard the skies. Through continuous monitoring and management of aircraft movements, these services ensure that the vast and complex airspace system operates smoothly, supporting the safe and timely transportation of millions of passengers and cargo every year.

Pilot/Controller Glossary

The Pilot/Controller Glossary serves as a comprehensive resource designed to standardize communications between pilots and air traffic controllers, ensuring clarity and reducing the potential for misunderstandings that could compromise safety. This glossary encompasses a wide array of terms, phrases, and acronyms pertinent to the operation within the National Airspace System (NAS). It is imperative for both pilots and controllers to have a profound understanding of this glossary, as it facilitates precise and effective communication, which is paramount in maintaining operational safety and efficiency.

Key terms within the glossary include, but are not limited to, "Acknowledged," which indicates that the pilot or controller has received the message and understands it, though it does not necessarily imply agreement with the instructions or information provided. "Altitude Restriction," a directive issued to maintain a specific altitude until further notice, underscores the critical nature of vertical separation for aircraft safety. "Cleared for Takeoff," signifies that the aircraft is authorized to commence its takeoff roll on the specified runway, indicating that the runway is free of known traffic and obstructions.

Further, "Direct Flight," refers to a flight path from one point to another without intermediate stops or deviations, optimizing efficiency and fuel consumption. "Emergency Frequency," a designated radio frequency such as 121.5 MHz for civil aviation, is used for emergency communications, highlighting the importance of having a universally recognized channel for distress signals. "Flight Plan," a document filed by a pilot or a dispatcher with the ATC, outlines the details of the planned flight or portion of a flight, assisting in traffic planning and management.

The term "IFR" (Instrument Flight Rules) denotes a set of regulations governing flight operations under conditions in which flight by outside visual reference is not safe. IFR operations require pilots to rely on cockpit instruments for navigation and control of the aircraft. Conversely, "VFR" (Visual Flight Rules) applies to regulations under which a pilot operates an aircraft in weather conditions generally clear enough to allow the pilot to see where the aircraft is going. Understanding the distinction between IFR and VFR is crucial for pilots and controllers to ensure the appropriate procedures are followed, enhancing safety and operational efficiency.

"Minimum En Route Altitude (MEA)," the lowest altitude between radio fixes that ensures acceptable navigational signal coverage and meets obstacle clearance requirements, exemplifies the intricate planning involved in route selection for safety and regulatory compliance. "NOTAM" (Notice to Airmen), a notice containing information essential to personnel concerned with flight operations but not known far enough in advance to be publicized by other means, is vital for the dissemination of temporary but critical information affecting flight safety.

The glossary also includes procedural terms such as "Roger," indicating that a transmission has been received and understood, and "Squawk," referring to a code assigned by air traffic control for an aircraft's transponder to transmit, aiding in the identification and tracking of the aircraft within radar systems.

Incorporating these terms and many others, the Pilot/Controller Glossary is an indispensable tool for enhancing mutual understanding and cooperation between pilots and air traffic controllers. Mastery of this glossary is essential for those operating within the NAS, as it not only contributes to individual proficiency but also to the collective safety and efficiency of airspace management. Through diligent study and application of this glossary, aviation professionals can ensure that their communications are precise, clear, and conducive to the safe conduct of flight operations.

Chapter 9: National Airspace System (NAS)

The National Airspace System (NAS) is a complex, interconnected network that encompasses the entirety of United States airspace and its associated infrastructure. This system is designed to ensure the safe and efficient movement of aircraft, both civilian and military, through a variety of airspace classifications and over vast geographical areas. The NAS integrates a wide range of components including airports, air traffic control facilities, navigation aids, and the rules and regulations that govern the use of airspace. Understanding the components of the NAS is crucial for all aviation professionals, as it forms the backbone of aviation operations within the United States.

Airports serve as critical nodes within the NAS, providing the infrastructure necessary for the takeoff, landing, and servicing of aircraft. These range from large international airports to smaller general aviation facilities, each playing a unique role in the overall system. Air traffic control facilities, including Terminal Radar Approach Control (TRACON) facilities, Air Route Traffic Control Centers (ARTCCs), and Air Traffic Control Towers (ATCTs), are tasked with managing the flow of air traffic within the NAS. These facilities use advanced radar and communication systems to ensure that aircraft are safely separated and efficiently routed through their respective sectors.

Navigation aids are another integral component of the NAS, providing pilots with the means to navigate accurately and safely from departure to destination. These aids include ground-based technologies such as VHF Omnidirectional Range (VOR) stations and Instrument Landing Systems (ILS), as well as satellite-based systems like the Global Positioning System (GPS). The integration of these navigation aids into the NAS allows for a variety of navigation and approach procedures to be employed, enhancing the flexibility and efficiency of flight operations.

The airspace within the NAS is divided into several classifications, each with its own set of rules and requirements. Controlled airspace, which includes Class A, B, C, D, and E airspace, requires aircraft to operate under the direction of air traffic control and adhere to specific entry, communication, and equipment requirements. Uncontrolled airspace, or Class G airspace, does not require such control, allowing for more flexibility in operations but also placing greater responsibility on pilots to ensure safety. Special use airspace, including restricted areas, military operation areas (MOAs), and temporary flight restrictions (TFRs), are designated for specific activities or to protect sensitive locations, and have additional access and operational restrictions.

The rules and regulations that govern the use of the NAS are codified in the Federal Aviation Regulations (FARs). These regulations establish the legal framework for aviation operations, setting forth the requirements for pilot certification, aircraft airworthiness, flight operations, and maintenance, among other areas. Compliance with the FARs is mandatory for all users of the NAS, ensuring that operations are conducted safely and in accordance with established standards.

The NAS is also supported by a range of services and technologies designed to enhance safety and efficiency. These include the Automatic Dependent Surveillance-Broadcast (ADS-B) system, which improves aircraft tracking and situational awareness, and the Traffic Collision Avoidance System (TCAS), which helps prevent mid-air collisions. Additionally, the NAS incorporates weather information services, providing pilots and air traffic controllers with critical data on weather conditions that may impact flight operations.

In summary, the National Airspace System is a comprehensive and multifaceted network that facilitates the safe and efficient movement of air traffic within the United States. Its components, including airports, air traffic control facilities, navigation aids, airspace classifications, and regulatory framework, are intricately linked to support a wide range of aviation activities. Understanding the NAS and its components is essential for aviation professionals, as it underpins the operations and procedures that ensure the safety and efficiency of flight in the national airspace.

Components of the NAS

The National Airspace System (NAS) is an intricate and comprehensive framework designed to accommodate the United States' airspace and its associated resources, facilitating not only the movement of civilian and military aircraft but also ensuring their safety and efficiency throughout operations. This system is a conglomeration of various components, each serving a pivotal role in the orchestration of airspace management, aircraft navigation, and the enforcement of regulations that govern air travel. Among these components, airports emerge as fundamental nodes, providing the essential infrastructure for aircraft operations including takeoffs, landings, and maintenance activities. These facilities vary in size and capacity, from sprawling international airports to smaller, regional airfields, each integrated into the NAS to support the diverse needs of the aviation community.

Air traffic control facilities, encompassing Terminal Radar Approach Control (TRACON) facilities, Air Route Traffic Control Centers (ARTCCs), and Air Traffic Control Towers (ATCTs), represent another critical component. These facilities are tasked with the management of air traffic flow, utilizing sophisticated radar and communication systems to monitor aircraft movements, ensuring safe separation and efficient routing. TRACON facilities focus on aircraft approaching or departing airports, ARTCCs manage en-route traffic across vast regions, and ATCTs oversee the immediate airspace around airports, including ground movements.

Navigation aids form an indispensable part of the NAS, offering pilots the tools necessary for precise navigation from departure to destination. These aids range from traditional ground-based systems, such as VHF Omnidirectional Range (VOR) stations and Instrument Landing Systems (ILS), to advanced satellite-based systems like the Global Positioning System (GPS). The integration of these aids facilitates a variety of navigation and approach procedures, enhancing the safety and efficiency of flight operations.

The airspace within the NAS is meticulously organized into several classifications, each defined by specific rules and operational requirements. Controlled airspace, categorized into Classes A, B, C, D, and E, mandates aircraft to adhere to air traffic control directives and comply with certain entry, communication, and equipment requirements. Conversely, Class G airspace, or uncontrolled airspace, offers more operational flexibility but places a greater onus on pilots to ensure safety. Additionally, special use airspace, including restricted areas, military operation areas (MOAs), and temporary flight restrictions (TFRs), are designated for particular activities or to safeguard sensitive locations, imposing further restrictions on access and operations.

The regulatory framework that underpins the NAS is encapsulated in the Federal Aviation Regulations (FARs), which delineate the legal requirements for aviation operations. These regulations cover a broad spectrum, from pilot certification and aircraft airworthiness to flight operations and maintenance, ensuring that all activities within the NAS conform to the highest standards of safety and legality.

Supporting the NAS are various services and technologies aimed at bolstering safety and operational efficiency. The Automatic Dependent Surveillance-Broadcast (ADS-B) system enhances aircraft tracking and situational awareness, while the Traffic Collision Avoidance System (TCAS) aids in preventing mid-air collisions. Weather information services also play a crucial role, providing pilots and air traffic controllers with vital data on weather conditions that could impact flight operations.

In essence, the National Airspace System represents a complex yet highly coordinated network that underlies the safe and efficient movement of air traffic within the United States. Its components, from airports and air traffic control facilities to navigation aids, airspace classifications, and regulatory frameworks, are interlinked to support a wide array of aviation activities. Understanding these components is essential for aviation professionals, as it forms the foundation upon which safe and efficient flight operations are conducted.

Special Use Airspace

Special Use Airspace encompasses regions of airspace with defined dimensions where activities must be confined because of their nature, limitations are imposed on aircraft operations that are not part of those activities, or both. These areas are designed to safeguard national security, protect the environment, manage air traffic flow, or ensure safety for ground-based activities such as rocket launches or military exercises. Understanding the classifications and restrictions of Special Use Airspace is crucial for pilots to navigate the National Airspace System (NAS) safely and efficiently.

Restricted Areas signify airspace within which the flight of aircraft, while not wholly prohibited, is subject to restrictions. Activities within these areas often involve hazardous operations, such as artillery firing, aerial gunnery, or guided missiles. Prior authorization from the controlling agency is required for entry, and pilots must be aware of the times of operation, which are typically published in the Chart Supplement U.S.

Prohibited Areas are defined spaces within which the flight of aircraft is prohibited. These areas are established for security or other reasons associated with the national welfare. Examples include airspace over the White House or certain military installations. The boundaries of Prohibited Areas are charted on aeronautical charts and listed in the Chart Supplement U.S.

Warning Areas are similar to Restricted Areas; however, they extend from three nautical miles outward from the coast of the United States into international airspace. Warning Areas inform pilots that they are entering an area containing activities that could be hazardous to non-participating aircraft. While flight is not prohibited, pilots should exercise caution.

Military Operation Areas (MOAs) are established to separate certain military training activities from IFR traffic. When MOAs are active, nonparticipating IFR traffic may be cleared through the area if ATC can provide the appropriate separation, or it may be rerouted. VFR pilots should exercise caution and contact any controlling agency for traffic advisories.

Alert Areas are designated to inform pilots of areas that may contain a high volume of pilot training or an unusual type of aerial activity. Both participating and nonparticipating pilots are responsible for collision avoidance.

Controlled Firing Areas (CFAs) are not charted because activities are suspended immediately when a spotter aircraft, radar, or ground lookout position indicates an aircraft might be approaching the area. Thus, CFAs do not cause nonparticipating aircraft to change their flight path.

National Security Areas (NSAs) consist of airspace of defined vertical and lateral dimensions established at locations where there is a requirement for increased security and safety of ground facilities. Pilots are requested to voluntarily avoid flying through the depicted NSA.

Understanding and respecting the boundaries and requirements of Special Use Airspace is essential for the safety and security of all airspace users.

Pilots must familiarize themselves with the locations, activating conditions, and restrictions of these areas through careful pre-flight planning and by consulting current aeronautical charts and publications. Compliance ensures not only the safety of the pilot and aircraft but also the integrity of national security and the safety of ground-based activities within these designated spaces.

Restricted Areas

Restricted Areas are delineated regions of airspace that present unique challenges and requirements for pilots due to the presence of hazardous activities such as military exercises, missile firing, or artillery training. These areas are not off-limits to all aircraft, but entry is controlled and subject to strict regulations. Pilots must obtain prior authorization from the controlling agency, which is typically the military or another governmental entity, to enter a Restricted Area. The operating hours and specific restrictions of these areas are published in the Chart Supplement U.S., and it is incumbent upon pilots to review this information during the pre-flight planning phase to ensure compliance and safety.

The dimensions of Restricted Areas are defined by vertical and lateral limits, providing pilots with clear boundaries to avoid unauthorized entry. These areas are charted on aeronautical charts, making it essential for pilots to familiarize themselves with chart symbols and legends to effectively identify Restricted Areas during flight planning and navigation. When planning a flight that may come into proximity with a Restricted Area, pilots should consult NOTAMs (Notices to Airmen) for any temporary changes to the status or dimensions of the area, as activities within Restricted Areas can fluctuate, leading to changes in their operational status.

For flights that necessitate transit through a Restricted Area, pilots must contact the controlling agency well in advance to request permission. The process for obtaining authorization can vary, and it may involve providing specific flight details such as the intended route, altitude, and time of entry. If permission is granted, pilots must adhere strictly to the agreed-upon route and instructions to ensure safety and compliance. Unauthorized entry into a Restricted Area can result in significant legal repercussions, including fines and suspension of pilot certificates, underscoring the importance of adherence to regulations.

In instances where a flight plan inadvertently includes passage through a Restricted Area without prior authorization, pilots are advised to immediately contact the nearest Air Traffic Control (ATC) facility for assistance in altering the flight path to avoid the restricted space. ATC can provide guidance and, if necessary, coordinate with the controlling agency to facilitate safe passage around or, in exceptional cases, through the Restricted Area.

The presence of Restricted Areas within the National Airspace System underscores the complex interplay between civil and military aviation needs. By respecting the boundaries and requirements of these areas, pilots contribute to the safety and security of all airspace users. It is through diligent pre-flight planning, ongoing communication with ATC, and adherence to established procedures that pilots can navigate around or gain authorized access to Restricted Areas, ensuring the safety of their flights and the integrity of national defense operations.

Military Operation Areas (MOAs)

Military Operation Areas (MOAs) serve a critical function within the National Airspace System by designating spaces where military training activities, such as air combat maneuvers, low-altitude tactics, and aerial refueling, can occur without interfering with civilian air traffic. These areas are delineated to ensure that military operations have the necessary airspace to conduct training while simultaneously safeguarding the integrity of civilian flight operations. MOAs are typically active during specific hours, which are published in aeronautical charts and the Chart Supplement U.S., allowing pilots to plan their flights with awareness of potential military activity.

When MOAs are active, the airspace within them is not restricted to civilian aircraft, but pilots flying under Visual Flight Rules (VFR) are advised to contact the controlling agency for traffic advisories. This communication is crucial for maintaining situational awareness and ensuring safety as it allows pilots to receive real-time information about military activities and other traffic within the MOA. For pilots operating under Instrument Flight

Rules (IFR), Air Traffic Control (ATC) may route flights through an MOA if it can ensure separation from military traffic. However, ATC may also reroute IFR traffic around active MOAs to avoid potential conflicts.

Understanding the operational status of MOAs is essential for flight planning. Pilots must consult NOTAMs (Notices to Airmen) for any temporary changes in MOA status, such as unscheduled activations or extensions of active periods. This information is vital for avoiding inadvertent entry into active military training spaces, which could pose safety risks due to the high-speed maneuvers and other specialized operations conducted by military aircraft.

Pilots navigating near or through MOAs should maintain a heightened level of vigilance, continuously monitor ATC communications, and be prepared for possible encounters with fast-moving military aircraft. The use of traffic collision avoidance systems (TCAS) and adherence to see-and-avoid principles are critical components of safe operations in these areas. Additionally, understanding the vertical and lateral boundaries of MOAs, as depicted on aeronautical charts, enables pilots to make informed decisions about altitude adjustments or course deviations that may be necessary to avoid active military operations.

The integration of MOAs within the National Airspace System underscores the collaborative efforts between civilian and military aviation authorities to ensure the safety and efficiency of all airspace users. By respecting the operational status of MOAs and adhering to recommended communication protocols, pilots contribute to a safe flying environment for both military and civilian aircraft. The proactive management of flight paths, combined with effective use of available navigational information, allows for the harmonious coexistence of diverse aviation activities within the shared airspace.

Chapter 10: Safety of Flight

Weather Minimums play a pivotal role in ensuring the safety of flight operations across various classes of airspace, necessitating pilots to possess a comprehensive understanding of these requirements to make informed decisions regarding flight planning and execution. Weather minimums are established to provide a buffer of safety by ensuring that pilots have sufficient visibility and cloud clearance to navigate by sight, which is critical for avoiding in-flight hazards such as terrain, other aircraft, and man-made obstacles. The Federal Aviation Regulations (FAR) specify different weather minimums for operations under Visual Flight Rules (VFR) and Instrument Flight Rules (IFR), tailored to the operational needs and safety considerations of each flight regime.

For VFR operations, the FAR delineates specific visibility and cloud clearance requirements that vary by airspace class. For instance, in Class B airspace, pilots must maintain clear of clouds and have 3 statute miles of visibility to operate, recognizing the high volume of traffic and the mix of VFR and IFR operations within this airspace. In contrast, Class C and D airspaces require pilots to maintain 1 statute mile of visibility and 500 feet below, 1,000 feet above, and 2,000 feet horizontally from clouds. These requirements ensure that pilots operating in the vicinity of airports with operational control towers have adequate visibility to see and avoid other aircraft and obstacles. Class E airspace, which serves as a controlled environment for IFR operations and extends down to the surface in designated areas to accommodate instrument approaches, requires 3 statute miles of visibility and cloud clearances similar to Class C and D airspaces for VFR flights. Uncontrolled Class G airspace has the most lenient weather minimums, recognizing the lower risk profile due to the absence of air traffic control services and typically lower volumes of traffic. During the day, pilots must maintain 1 statute mile of visibility and clear of clouds when operating below 1,200 feet above ground level (AGL) in Class G airspace, with increased visibility and cloud clearance requirements at higher altitudes to mitigate the risk of collision with other aircraft operating under IFR.

Pilots operating under IFR, in contrast, are not subject to the same visibility and cloud clearance requirements as VFR pilots because they rely on aircraft instruments and air traffic control guidance to navigate. However, understanding the weather minimums for IFR operations is crucial for flight planning and decision-making. IFR weather minimums are primarily concerned with the minimum visibility and cloud ceiling required for aircraft to conduct instrument approaches to airports. These minimums vary depending on the type of approach and the specific procedures for each airport, with precision approaches generally allowing lower minimums than non-precision approaches due to the enhanced navigational guidance they provide. Pilots must consult the appropriate approach plates for the airports they intend to use to determine the applicable weather minimums for their planned operations.

Adherence to weather minimums is a critical component of flight safety, requiring pilots to accurately interpret weather reports and forecasts during pre-flight planning and to continuously monitor weather conditions during flight. Pilots must be prepared to alter their flight plans or seek alternate destinations if weather conditions deteriorate below the prescribed minimums, prioritizing safety over convenience or expediency. The ability to make sound decisions based on weather conditions and to operate within the established weather minimums is a hallmark of airmanship and is essential for the safe conduct of both VFR and IFR flights.

To assess understanding of weather minimums, consider the following multiple-choice questions:

1. What is the minimum visibility requirement for VFR flight in Class B airspace?
[A] 1 statute mile
[B] 3 statute miles
[C] 5 statute miles
[D] Clear of clouds

2. Which airspace requires pilots to maintain 500 feet below, 1,000 feet above, and 2,000 feet horizontally from clouds for VFR operations?
[A] Class A
[B] Class B
[C] Class C and D
[D] Class G

3. For IFR operations, where can pilots find the specific weather minimums required for instrument approaches at their destination airport?

[A] In the FAR
[B] On the weather briefing
[C] On the approach plates
[D] In the Aeronautical Information Manual

These questions underscore the importance of understanding and applying weather minimums as part of the pre-flight planning process and in-flight decision-making to ensure the safety of flight operations across different classes of airspace.

Weather Minimums

Weather minimums are critical parameters that dictate the conditions under which pilots can safely operate aircraft in various classes of airspace. These minimums are designed to ensure that pilots have adequate visibility and cloud clearance to navigate effectively, thus preventing collisions and maintaining the safety of flight operations. The Federal Aviation Administration (FAA) has established specific weather minimums for both Visual Flight Rules (VFR) and Instrument Flight Rules (IFR) operations, which are detailed in the Federal Aviation Regulations (FAR). For VFR flights, weather minimums vary significantly depending on the class of airspace in which the aircraft is operating. In Class B airspace, known for its high volume of air traffic and mix of VFR and IFR operations, pilots are required to maintain clear of clouds with a minimum of 3 statute miles of visibility. This ensures that pilots have sufficient visibility to see and avoid other aircraft as well as navigate around obstacles. Class C and D airspaces, which surround airports with operational control towers, require 1 statute mile of visibility and specific cloud clearances: 500 feet below, 1,000 feet above, and 2,000 feet horizontally from clouds. These requirements are designed to facilitate the safe coexistence of VFR and IFR operations in the vicinity of airports. Class E airspace, which accommodates a controlled environment for IFR operations as well as VFR flights, mandates 3 statute miles of visibility and similar cloud clearances to Classes C and D for VFR operations. The least restrictive weather minimums are found in Class G airspace, an uncontrolled airspace where the risk profile is lower due to the absence of air traffic control services. During the day, VFR flights below 1,200 feet above ground level (AGL) in Class G airspace must maintain 1 statute mile of visibility and remain clear of clouds, with requirements increasing at higher altitudes to ensure safety among potentially mixed VFR and IFR traffic.

IFR operations, which allow pilots to fly primarily by reference to instruments and rely on air traffic control for navigation assistance, have their own set of weather minimums. These minimums are not based on visibility and cloud clearance in the same way as VFR minimums but instead focus on the minimum visibility and cloud ceiling required for the safe completion of instrument approaches at airports. IFR weather minimums vary depending on the type of instrument approach procedure being executed, with precision approaches generally allowing for lower minimums due to the higher accuracy of navigational guidance available. Pilots must refer to the specific approach plates for their destination airports to determine the exact weather minimums applicable to their intended operations. Compliance with weather minimums is not only a regulatory requirement but also a critical aspect of risk management in flight operations. Pilots must exercise due diligence in pre-flight planning by reviewing weather forecasts and reports to ensure that the anticipated weather conditions meet or exceed the prescribed minimums for their intended flight path and operations. In-flight vigilance is equally important as weather conditions can change rapidly, necessitating possible adjustments to the flight plan to maintain compliance with weather minimums. The FAA provides various resources, including the Aviation Weather Center and Flight Service Stations, to assist pilots in obtaining accurate and up-to-date weather information.

To reinforce the understanding of weather minimums, consider the following multiple-choice questions:

1. What is the minimum cloud clearance requirement for VFR flight in Class C airspace?
[A] Clear of clouds
[B] 500 feet below, 1,000 feet above, and 2,000 feet horizontally from clouds
[C] 1,000 feet below, 1,000 feet above, and 1 mile horizontally from clouds
[D] No specific cloud clearance requirement

2. In which class of airspace are VFR flights allowed the least restrictive weather minimums during the day below 1,200 feet AGL?
[A] Class A
[B] Class B

[C] Class C
[D] Class G

3. Where can pilots find the specific IFR weather minimums required for instrument approaches at their destination airport?
[A] In the FAR
[B] On the weather briefing
[C] On the approach plates
[D] In the Aeronautical Information Manual

These questions highlight the importance of understanding the specific weather minimums applicable to different classes of airspace and operations. Mastery of this knowledge enables pilots to plan and conduct flights safely, adhering to the regulatory requirements and mitigating the risks associated with adverse weather conditions.

Collision Avoidance

Question: When flying under VFR in class E airspace, what is the minimum safe altitude for aircraft to ensure collision avoidance over congested areas?

- A) An altitude allowing, if a power unit fails, an emergency landing without undue hazard to persons or property on the surface.
- B) An altitude of 1,000 feet above the highest obstacle within a horizontal radius of 2,000 feet of the aircraft.
- C) An altitude of 500 feet above the surface, except over open water or sparsely populated areas.

Correct answer explanation: B) An altitude of 1,000 feet above the highest obstacle within a horizontal radius of 2,000 feet of the aircraft.

According to Federal Aviation Regulations, when flying under Visual Flight Rules (VFR) in class E airspace over congested areas, the minimum safe altitude is one that allows for an emergency landing without undue hazard to persons or property on the surface, should a power unit fail. Specifically, the regulation states that over congested areas, an aircraft must maintain an altitude of 1,000 feet above the highest obstacle within a horizontal radius of 2,000 feet of the aircraft. This rule is designed to ensure that, in the event of an emergency, the pilot has sufficient altitude and space to maneuver for a safe landing, thereby minimizing the risk of collision with any obstacles or causing harm to people and property on the ground. This regulation underscores the importance of maintaining situational awareness and planning flights to adhere to safe altitude guidelines, thus significantly contributing to collision avoidance.

Wake Turbulence Avoidance

Wake turbulence, a phenomenon produced by the passage of an aircraft through the atmosphere, poses significant risks to aircraft, particularly during takeoff and landing phases. Generated by the lift created by the wings of an aircraft, wake turbulence consists of two counter-rotating vortices trailing from the wingtips. The strength of these vortices is directly related to the weight, speed, and wing shape of the generating aircraft, with larger, heavier aircraft producing more potent wake turbulence. Understanding and avoiding wake turbulence is crucial for maintaining flight safety, especially for smaller aircraft that are more susceptible to the effects of these vortices.

To mitigate the risk of wake turbulence encounters, pilots must adhere to specific operational procedures and separation standards. During takeoff and landing, air traffic controllers apply increased separation between heavy or large aircraft and following lighter aircraft to allow wake turbulence to dissipate or drift away from the flight path of the trailing aircraft. Pilots can also employ tactical strategies when operating in conditions where wake turbulence is a concern. For instance, during takeoff, a pilot should aim to rotate and lift off before the point where the preceding aircraft became airborne and climb above its flight path. Conversely, during landing, the objective is to remain above the glide path of the preceding aircraft and touch down beyond its touchdown point, thus avoiding the wake turbulence that may linger in the descent path.

In-flight avoidance of wake turbulence involves maintaining lateral separation from the flight paths of larger aircraft, particularly when operating in visual meteorological conditions (VMC) where pilots can visually identify and steer clear of potential wake turbulence sources. Additionally, understanding the behavior of wake vortices under various atmospheric conditions is essential. For example, vortices tend to sink and move laterally in calm air, but in windy conditions, they may drift downwind, altering the areas of potential turbulence. Pilots must be vigilant and adjust their flight paths accordingly to maintain safe distances from these invisible hazards.

The importance of pilot education on wake turbulence cannot be overstated. Training programs and recurrent training sessions should emphasize the dynamics of wake turbulence, recognition of hazardous situations, and the application of avoidance techniques. Simulation and practical exercises can enhance a pilot's ability to recognize and react appropriately to wake turbulence encounters, thereby reducing the risk of loss of control or structural damage to the aircraft.

To evaluate the understanding of wake turbulence avoidance, consider the following multiple-choice questions:

1. What factor primarily determines the strength of wake turbulence generated by an aircraft?
[A] The color of the aircraft
[B] The weight, speed, and wing shape of the aircraft
[C] The altitude at which the aircraft is flying
[D] The number of engines on the aircraft

2. Which of the following is a recommended practice for a pilot taking off after a heavy aircraft?
[A] Take off well before the rotation point of the preceding aircraft
[B] Rotate and lift off before the point where the preceding aircraft became airborne
[C] Follow the exact flight path of the preceding aircraft to stay in its wake
[D] Delay takeoff for at least 30 minutes to allow wake turbulence to dissipate

3. During landing, how should a pilot approach the runway to avoid wake turbulence if following a larger aircraft?
[A] Land before the touchdown point of the preceding aircraft
[B] Remain above the glide path of the preceding aircraft and touch down beyond its touchdown point
[C] Aim to land at the same touchdown point as the preceding aircraft for efficiency
[D] Fly lower than the glide path of the preceding aircraft to avoid its wake turbulence

These questions underscore the critical nature of wake turbulence awareness and the implementation of avoidance strategies to ensure the safety of flight operations. By adhering to recommended separation distances and employing tactical flight maneuvers, pilots can effectively minimize the risks associated with wake turbulence.

Chapter 11: Security

TSA Regulations and Guidelines play a pivotal role in ensuring the security of all aviation operations, affecting passengers, cargo, and the aviation workforce alike. These regulations are designed to safeguard against acts of terrorism, hijacking, and other security threats that could compromise the safety of air travel. The Transportation Security Administration (TSA) has established a comprehensive framework of rules and procedures that are enforced at airports, in air traffic, and within all sectors of the aviation industry. One of the key aspects of TSA regulations is the stringent screening process for passengers and their baggage. This includes the use of advanced imaging technology, metal detectors, and physical inspections to detect prohibited items such as weapons, explosives, and other hazardous materials. Passengers are required to comply with the TSA's 3-1-1 liquid rule for carry-ons, ensuring that liquids, gels, aerosols, creams, and pastes are packed in accordance with the guidelines to expedite the screening process and enhance security measures.

Cargo security is another critical component of TSA regulations, involving rigorous inspection and certification processes for all cargo transported on passenger and cargo aircraft. The TSA employs a multi-layered approach to cargo security, including known shipper programs, canine screening, and advanced technology inspections to prevent unauthorized materials and substances from being transported by air. The Air Cargo Advance Screening (ACAS) program further enhances security by requiring the submission of detailed cargo information before loading onto the aircraft, allowing for targeted inspections based on risk assessments.

For aviation employees, including pilots, flight attendants, and ground crew, the TSA mandates thorough background checks and security training to ensure that individuals with access to secure areas of airports and aircraft do not pose a threat to aviation security. The Secure Identification Display Area (SIDA) badges are issued to personnel after verifying their identity and assessing their background, granting them access to restricted areas based on their role and necessity.

The TSA also oversees the Federal Flight Deck Officer (FFDO) program, which trains and authorizes flight crew members to carry firearms and defend the cockpit against hostile actions. This program is part of a broader effort to reinforce the security of the flight deck and deter potential threats to commercial flights.

In addition to these measures, the TSA collaborates with other federal agencies and international partners to enhance global aviation security standards, sharing intelligence and best practices to prevent and respond to emerging threats. The TSA's guidelines for passengers, including recommendations for packing, identification requirements, and procedures for special situations such as traveling with children or medical conditions, are regularly updated to reflect current security concerns and technological advancements.

To assess understanding of TSA regulations and guidelines, consider the following multiple-choice questions:

1. What is the purpose of the TSA's 3-1-1 liquid rule for carry-on baggage?
[A] To limit the volume of liquids for environmental reasons
[B] To expedite the screening process and enhance security measures
[C] To reduce the weight of carry-on baggage on aircraft
[D] To encourage passengers to check more baggage

2. Which program requires the submission of detailed cargo information before loading onto an aircraft?
[A] Known Shipper Program
[B] Canine Screening Program
[C] Air Cargo Advance Screening (ACAS) program
[D] Secure Freight Initiative

3. What is the primary role of the Federal Flight Deck Officer (FFDO) program?
[A] To provide flight crew members with first aid training
[B] To train and authorize flight crew members to carry firearms and defend the cockpit
[C] To certify pilots in advanced navigation systems
[D] To conduct background checks on flight crew members

These questions highlight the multifaceted approach of TSA regulations and guidelines in maintaining the security of the aviation sector, emphasizing the importance of compliance and awareness among all stakeholders in the aviation community. Through rigorous enforcement of these regulations and continuous adaptation to evolving security threats, the TSA strives to ensure the safety and security of air travel for passengers, cargo, and the aviation workforce.

TSA Regulations and Guidelines

The Transportation Security Administration (TSA) plays a crucial role in maintaining the security of the aviation sector through the implementation of comprehensive regulations and guidelines designed to protect passengers, crew, and infrastructure from potential threats. These measures encompass a wide range of procedures, from passenger and baggage screening to cargo inspection and the vetting of aviation employees. The TSA's approach is characterized by its adaptability, employing both established and emerging technologies to respond to evolving security challenges. One of the foundational elements of TSA's security measures is the rigorous screening process that all passengers and their baggage undergo before boarding an aircraft. This process utilizes advanced imaging technology, metal detectors, and manual checks to identify and prevent prohibited items, such as weapons, explosives, and other dangerous objects, from being brought onto aircraft. The effectiveness of this screening process is enhanced by the TSA's 3-1-1 rule for liquids, gels, aerosols, creams, and pastes in carry-on baggage, which streamlines the screening process and minimizes the risk of these items being used to compromise aircraft security.

Cargo security represents another critical facet of TSA's regulatory framework. The TSA mandates that all cargo transported on passenger and cargo aircraft undergo thorough inspection to prevent the carriage of unauthorized materials. This is achieved through a multi-layered strategy that includes physical inspections, canine detection teams, and the use of advanced screening technologies. The Air Cargo Advance Screening (ACAS) program exemplifies TSA's proactive approach to cargo security, requiring the submission of detailed cargo information prior to loading onto an aircraft for targeted risk assessments and inspections.

The vetting of aviation employees is equally stringent, with the TSA requiring comprehensive background checks and security training for all individuals with access to secure areas of airports and aircraft. This ensures that those who have direct contact with the aviation infrastructure or passengers do not pose a security threat. The issuance of Secure

Identification Display Area (SIDA) badges, following identity verification and background assessment, controls access to restricted areas, allowing only authorized personnel to enter.

The Federal Flight Deck Officer (FFDO) program underscores the TSA's commitment to reinforcing the security of the flight deck. Through this program, selected flight crew members are trained and authorized to carry firearms to defend the cockpit against hostile actions, serving as a last line of defense in the event of an attempt to compromise the cockpit.

Collaboration and information sharing with other federal agencies and international partners are vital components of TSA's strategy to enhance global aviation security standards. This cooperative approach facilitates the exchange of intelligence and best practices, enabling the TSA to stay ahead of emerging threats and continuously refine its security measures.

The TSA also provides comprehensive guidelines for passengers to ensure smooth compliance with security procedures. These guidelines cover a range of topics, from packing recommendations to identification requirements and procedures for special situations such as traveling with children or medical conditions. Regular updates to these guidelines reflect the TSA's commitment to adapting its security measures in response to new threats and technological advancements.

Multiple-choice questions to assess understanding of TSA regulations and guidelines might include:

1. What is the primary goal of the TSA's passenger and baggage screening process?
[A] To ensure that flights depart on schedule
[B] To detect and prevent prohibited items from being brought onto aircraft
[C] To collect data on passenger travel habits
[D] To provide employment opportunities in the security sector

2. How does the Air Cargo Advance Screening (ACAS) program enhance cargo security?
[A] By requiring physical inspection of all cargo items
[B] By mandating that cargo be shipped in tamper-evident packaging
[C] By requiring the submission of detailed cargo information before loading onto an aircraft
[D] By implementing a global tracking system for all cargo shipments

3. What is the purpose of the Federal Flight Deck Officer (FFDO) program?
[A] To provide flight crew members with advanced navigation training
[B] To train and authorize flight crew members to carry firearms and defend the cockpit
[C] To conduct background checks on all flight crew members
[D] To certify flight crew members in emergency medical procedures

Through the implementation of these regulations and guidelines, the TSA ensures the security of the aviation sector, protecting passengers, crew, and infrastructure from potential threats while facilitating the safe and efficient movement of people and goods by air.

Security Control of Air Traffic

Security control of air traffic plays a pivotal role in maintaining the safety and integrity of the National Airspace System (NAS). This involves a comprehensive set of measures, protocols, and regulations designed to protect air traffic from acts of unlawful interference, ensuring that both passengers and cargo reach their destinations without compromise to their safety. The Transportation Security Administration (TSA), in collaboration with the Federal Aviation Administration (FAA), oversees the implementation of these security measures, which include but are not limited to the screening of passengers and baggage, securing cockpit access, and the monitoring of aircraft while in flight and on the ground.

One of the critical components of air traffic security is the vetting of passengers through the Secure Flight program. This program cross-references passenger information against watchlists to identify individuals who may pose a threat to aviation security. Airlines are required to collect specific information from passengers and transmit it to the TSA for this purpose. The effectiveness of Secure Flight underscores the importance of accurate and timely data collection and sharing among various stakeholders in the aviation sector.

Another significant aspect of air traffic security is the Air Marshal Service, which places armed federal air marshals on select flights to deter and counteract hijackings and other terrorist acts. These marshals are trained in crisis management, negotiation, and advanced combat techniques, providing an essential layer of security for high-risk flights.

The FAA also mandates strict access control measures at airports to prevent unauthorized entry to sensitive areas such as the tarmac, cargo handling, and maintenance facilities. These measures include biometric identification systems, security badges, and surveillance cameras, which work in tandem to secure critical infrastructure from potential threats.

In addition to physical security measures, cybersecurity protocols are in place to protect the communication and information systems that air traffic control relies on. The increasing reliance on digital technologies in aviation has made cybersecurity a top priority, with continuous efforts to safeguard against hacking, data breaches, and other cyber threats that could disrupt air traffic control operations.

Collaboration between various government agencies and the aviation industry is crucial to the ongoing enhancement of air traffic security. Regular training exercises, security audits, and the sharing of intelligence and best practices are essential components of a robust security strategy. These collaborative efforts ensure that security measures are not only reactive but also proactive, adapting to emerging threats and incorporating advancements in technology.

The responsibility for air traffic security extends beyond government agencies and the aviation industry. Passengers play a vital role by adhering to security protocols, reporting suspicious activities, and cooperating with security personnel. This collective approach to security underscores the shared commitment to safe and secure air travel, reinforcing the notion that the safety of the skies is a paramount concern that requires vigilance and cooperation from all parties involved.

In essence, the security control of air traffic is a multifaceted endeavor that integrates advanced technology, stringent regulations, and international cooperation to safeguard the aviation sector from evolving threats. Through continuous improvement and adaptation of security measures, the FAA, TSA, and their partners strive to maintain a secure environment for air travel, ensuring that the freedom of the skies remains protected against unlawful interference.

Chapter 12: Pilot's Bill of Rights

The Pilot's Bill of Rights (PBoR) was enacted to ensure that pilots are afforded protection and fair treatment during enforcement actions by the Federal Aviation Administration (FAA) and other aviation authorities. This legislation is critical for pilots to understand, as it directly impacts their rights and responsibilities in the event of an investigation or enforcement action. The PBoR provides several key protections, including the right to be notified of any investigation, the right to access air traffic data, and the right to a fair hearing.

One of the foundational aspects of the PBoR is the requirement for the FAA to notify pilots in writing of any investigation that could result in an enforcement action. This notification must include a description of the incident or violation under investigation and must be provided in a timely manner, allowing pilots adequate time to prepare a response or defense. This ensures transparency in the FAA's enforcement process and gives pilots the opportunity to correct any misunderstandings or discrepancies before formal action is taken.

Another significant provision within the PBoR is the right of pilots to obtain air traffic data related to an investigation. This data can include recordings of ATC communications, radar information, and other relevant data that can be crucial for a pilot's defense. Access to this data allows pilots to review the facts of the case from the FAA's perspective and to challenge or corroborate the evidence against them. It is important for pilots to request this data as soon as they are notified of an investigation to ensure they have sufficient time to review and utilize the information in their defense.

The PBoR also guarantees pilots the right to a fair trial, including the option to have their case heard by an administrative law judge at the National Transportation Safety Board (NTSB). This provision ensures that pilots have an opportunity to present evidence, call witnesses, and cross-examine FAA witnesses in a formal legal setting. The NTSB judge's decision can then be appealed to the full NTSB board and, if necessary, to a federal court, providing multiple levels of review to safeguard pilots' rights.

In addition to these protections, the PBoR mandates improvements in the FAA's notification and reporting processes, aiming to increase transparency and accountability within the agency. The FAA is required to provide comprehensive information about the nature of the investigation, the specific regulations allegedly violated, and the evidence supporting the FAA's findings. This level of detail is intended to help pilots better understand the allegations against them and to prepare a more effective defense.

Understanding the provisions of the Pilot's Bill of Rights is essential for all pilots, as it directly affects their legal protections and procedural rights during FAA enforcement actions. Pilots should familiarize themselves with the PBoR and consider consulting with an aviation attorney if they are subject to an FAA investigation or enforcement action. By being informed and proactive, pilots can better navigate the complexities of FAA regulations and enforcement procedures, ensuring their rights are protected throughout the process.

Notification of Investigation

Upon receiving a notification of investigation from the Federal Aviation Administration (FAA), pilots are immediately thrust into a procedural environment that demands meticulous attention to detail and a comprehensive understanding of their rights under the Pilot's Bill of Rights (PBoR). The initial notification serves as the formal commencement of the FAA's investigative process, a critical juncture at which the pilot's response—or lack thereof—can significantly influence the outcome of the investigation. It is imperative for pilots to recognize the gravity of this notification and to undertake immediate, informed action to safeguard their interests and aviation career.

The notification letter typically outlines the nature of the alleged violation or incident under scrutiny, providing the pilot with a preliminary understanding of the FAA's concerns. This communication is not merely informational but serves as a legal trigger that activates the pilot's rights under the PBoR, including the right to obtain air traffic data and other evidence pertinent to the FAA's investigation. Pilots should, therefore, scrutinize the notification letter for specific details regarding the alleged incident, including the date, location, and nature of the purported violation. This information is crucial for formulating an effective response strategy and for requesting relevant air traffic data that may exonerate the pilot or clarify the circumstances surrounding the incident.

In responding to the notification of investigation, pilots must adhere to a strategic approach that encompasses several key actions. First and foremost, it is advisable to consult with an aviation attorney who specializes in FAA enforcement actions. Legal counsel can provide invaluable guidance on the nuances of the PBoR, assist in the collection and analysis of air traffic data, and represent the pilot in communications with the FAA. This professional assistance is particularly crucial in complex cases or when the pilot disputes the FAA's allegations.

Simultaneously, pilots should initiate a request for air traffic data related to the investigation, leveraging their right under the PBoR to access this information. This request should be made promptly to ensure that the data is preserved and made available for review. Air traffic data, including ATC communications, radar tracks, and other flight information, can be instrumental in corroborating the pilot's account of the incident or in identifying discrepancies in the FAA's allegations.

Throughout the investigative process, pilots must maintain meticulous records of all communications with the FAA and other relevant entities. This includes correspondence related to the notification of investigation, requests for air traffic data, and any other interactions pertaining to the case. Detailed record-keeping not only facilitates effective case management but also ensures that the pilot has a comprehensive dossier of evidence and documentation to support their defense.

Moreover, pilots should undertake a thorough review of the relevant Federal Aviation Regulations (FAR) cited in the notification of investigation. A deep understanding of these regulations and their applicability to the alleged incident is essential for crafting a cogent response to the FAA's allegations. This review may reveal regulatory nuances or exceptions that could mitigate the severity of the alleged violation or exculpate the pilot altogether.

In preparing their response to the FAA, pilots should articulate a clear, factual account of the incident, supported by evidence and a reasoned argument that addresses the specifics of the FAA's allegations. This response should be crafted in consultation with legal counsel to ensure that it effectively communicates the pilot's position while adhering to the procedural requirements of the FAA's investigative process.

The notification of investigation is a pivotal moment in the FAA's enforcement framework, setting the stage for the pilot's defense and the subsequent resolution of the case. By understanding their rights under the PBoR and taking proactive, informed steps in response to the FAA's notification, pilots can navigate the complexities of the investigative process with confidence, aiming for a favorable outcome that preserves their professional standing and aviation privileges.

Enforcement Actions

Enforcement actions within the realm of Federal Aviation Administration (FAA) oversight are critical mechanisms to ensure adherence to the established Federal Aviation Regulations (FAR). These actions are initiated when there is evidence or suspicion of non-compliance with the regulatory standards set forth to safeguard both the integrity of the National Airspace System (NAS) and the safety of the public. The spectrum of enforcement actions ranges from administrative remedies such as warnings and letters of correction, which are designed to educate and correct minor infractions, to more severe legal penalties including fines, suspension, or revocation of pilot certificates.

The process of enforcement is meticulously structured to ensure fairness and transparency, adhering to the principles outlined in the Pilot's Bill of Rights (PBoR). When the FAA identifies a potential violation, it embarks on a thorough investigation process, gathering evidence, and evaluating the circumstances surrounding the alleged non-compliance. This phase is crucial, as it determines the course of action the FAA will take. Should the evidence substantiate the violation, the FAA issues a notice of proposed enforcement action to the involved party, detailing the specific regulations violated and the proposed penalty.

Respondents to a notice of proposed enforcement action have the right to contest the FAA's findings and the proposed penalty. This is where the procedural safeguards provided by the PBoR become particularly significant. Pilots or other certificate holders have the option to engage in an informal conference with the FAA, presenting their case and any mitigating factors or evidence that may influence the outcome of the enforcement action. This step serves as a critical juncture, offering an opportunity for resolution without proceeding to formal legal action.

Should the matter not be resolved through informal means, it progresses to a formal hearing before an administrative law judge at the National Transportation Safety Board (NTSB). This hearing is a formal legal proceeding where both the FAA and the respondent present their cases, including evidence, witness testimony, and legal arguments. The administrative law judge then issues a decision based on the merits of the case, which can be appealed to the full NTSB board and, subsequently, to the federal court system if necessary.

The enforcement action process underscores the FAA's commitment to maintaining the highest standards of safety and compliance within the aviation community. It also highlights the importance of the PBoR in ensuring that those subject to enforcement actions are afforded due process and the opportunity to defend against allegations of regulatory violations. Pilots and other certificate holders are encouraged to familiarize themselves with both the FAR and the PBoR to fully understand their rights and responsibilities within the regulatory framework of aviation in the United States. This knowledge is not only crucial for navigating the enforcement action process but also for fostering a culture of compliance and safety within the aviation community.

Chapter 13: FAR/AIM Index

The FAR/AIM Index serves as a comprehensive navigational tool designed to facilitate quick and efficient access to specific regulations, guidelines, and operational procedures critical for pilots, aviation professionals, and enthusiasts. This meticulously organized index is structured to enhance the user's ability to locate pertinent information with ease, thereby supporting informed decision-making and compliance with federal aviation standards. The index is alphabetically arranged, covering a wide array of topics from air traffic control communications to weather minimums, ensuring a broad spectrum of aviation-related subjects is addressed. Each entry within the index is accompanied by a precise reference, pointing to the section or page number where the detailed discussion of the topic can be found, streamlining the process of sourcing information.

For instance, under the letter "A," one would find entries for "Air Traffic Control (ATC) Services and Communications," directing the reader to the specific chapter and section where comprehensive coverage of ATC protocols, procedures, and communication guidelines are elaborated. Similarly, entries such as "Medical Certificates" guide users to the sections detailing the requirements, processes, and standards for obtaining and maintaining medical certification as mandated by the Federal Aviation Administration (FAA).

The index also includes references to critical safety protocols, such as "Collision Avoidance" and "Wake Turbulence Avoidance," providing direct links to the sections where these vital safety measures are discussed in depth. This ensures that users seeking information on maintaining safety and compliance in various flight operations can quickly locate the necessary guidelines and procedures.

Furthermore, the FAR/AIM Index incorporates references to the "Pilot's Bill of Rights," offering immediate access to the sections that discuss the legal protections and procedural rights afforded to pilots under this legislation. This feature of the index is particularly beneficial for pilots navigating the complexities of FAA investigations and enforcement actions, as it provides a direct pathway to the information required to understand and exercise their rights effectively.

In addition to regulatory and procedural topics, the index encompasses entries on practical exercises and simulations, such as "Calculating Weight and Balance," "Reading and Interpreting METARs and TAFs," and "Planning a Cross-Country Flight under VFR/IFR." These entries direct readers to the sections where practical guidance, exercises, and scenarios are presented, supporting the application of theoretical knowledge in real-world contexts.

The FAR/AIM Index is an indispensable resource for anyone engaged in or interested in aviation, offering a structured and user-friendly means of accessing a wealth of information essential for safe, compliant, and efficient aviation operations. Its comprehensive coverage and organized format make it an invaluable tool for enhancing understanding, supporting compliance, and facilitating operational excellence in the field of aviation.

Using the Index

To effectively utilize the FAR/AIM Index, readers should first identify the specific topic or regulation of interest. The index is alphabetically organized, making it straightforward to navigate through various subjects. Upon locating the desired entry, note the accompanying reference which directs to the section or page number where detailed information on the topic can be found. This system is designed to streamline the process of accessing precise data, ensuring that users can quickly find the regulatory guidance or procedural details they require for their specific aviation-related queries or needs.

For efficient use, it is advisable to familiarize oneself with the general layout and categorization of topics within the index. This familiarity will significantly reduce the time spent searching for information and increase the overall utility of the document as a reference tool. Should the index be used in a digital format, utilizing the search function can expedite finding relevant entries. However, in both digital and print formats, taking the time to understand the structure and organization of the index will enhance the user's ability to leverage this resource effectively.

When consulting the index for regulatory information, it is crucial to cross-reference the identified section with the main body of the FAR/AIM to ensure a comprehensive understanding of the context and applicability of the regulation. This practice is particularly important as regulations may have nuances or exceptions that are detailed in the broader discussion within the main text. Additionally, for those seeking to deepen their knowledge or apply the information in practical scenarios, it is beneficial to explore related topics or sections suggested by the index. This approach not only broadens one's understanding of specific regulations but also provides a more holistic view of aviation operations and safety protocols.

In summary, the FAR/AIM Index is a meticulously organized tool designed to facilitate efficient access to a wide range of aviation regulations and guidelines. By adopting a methodical approach to its use, individuals can significantly enhance their research efficiency and regulatory comprehension, supporting informed decision-making and compliance in aviation activities.

Key Topics and Regulations

The Federal Aviation Regulations (FAR) and Aeronautical Information Manual (AIM) serve as the cornerstone for aviation safety, compliance, and operations within the United States. These documents are meticulously crafted to ensure that pilots, air traffic controllers, and other aviation professionals have access to the most current and comprehensive guidelines necessary for the safe and efficient use of the National Airspace System (NAS). Among the myriad of topics covered, several key areas stand out due to their critical importance in daily aviation operations. These include airspace classification, pilot certification requirements, aircraft maintenance protocols, and safety procedures, each of which is governed by specific regulations that are essential for adherence to federal aviation standards.

Airspace classification is delineated into various categories, from Class A to Class G, with each class having distinct operating rules, requirements, and procedures. This classification system is designed to facilitate a safe and orderly flow of air traffic, with Class A airspace being at the highest level, typically starting from 18,000 feet mean sea level (MSL) up to and including flight level 600, and reserved exclusively for instrument flight rules (IFR) operations. On the other end of the spectrum, Class G airspace is uncontrolled and encompasses the airspace from the surface to the base of the overlying Class E airspace. Understanding the nuances of each airspace class, including entry requirements, weather minimums, and equipment requirements, is paramount for pilots to navigate the NAS safely and efficiently.

Pilot certification is another area of significant importance, with the FAR outlining specific eligibility requirements, training standards, and examination procedures for various levels of pilot licenses and ratings. From the initial medical examination to the issuance of a pilot certificate, each step is governed by detailed regulations aimed at ensuring that pilots possess the necessary knowledge, skills, and experience to operate aircraft safely. The certification process includes passing written exams, accumulating a certain amount of flight hours, and demonstrating proficiency through practical tests administered by designated pilot examiners (DPEs).

Aircraft maintenance, repair, and alterations are regulated areas critical to the safety and airworthiness of the aviation fleet. The FAR mandates regular inspections, including annual and 100-hour inspections for certain aircraft, to ensure that all aircraft meet strict safety standards. Additionally, the regulations outline the scope of preventive maintenance tasks that can be performed by pilots and the requirements for more extensive repairs and alterations, which must be carried out by certified mechanics or repair stations. Keeping accurate and up-to-date maintenance records is also a regulatory requirement, providing a comprehensive history of each aircraft's maintenance, repairs, and alterations.

Safety procedures encompass a broad range of topics, from emergency operations and collision avoidance to security measures and hazardous materials handling. These procedures are designed to mitigate risks and enhance the safety of flight operations, both in the air and on the ground. The AIM provides detailed guidance on best practices and recommended procedures for dealing with various safety-related scenarios, complementing the regulatory mandates outlined in the FAR.

In addition to these key areas, the FAR/AIM also addresses numerous other aspects of aviation, including but not limited to air traffic control communications, weather services, navigational aids, and special use airspace. Each topic is accompanied by specific regulations and guidelines that collectively ensure the safe, efficient, and secure operation of the NAS. As the aviation industry continues to evolve, these regulations and guidelines are periodically reviewed and updated to reflect new technologies, operational practices, and safety findings, underscoring the dynamic nature of aviation regulation and the ongoing commitment to maintaining the highest standards of safety and compliance in the aviation community.

Chapter 14: Practical Exercises

Understanding NOTAMs (Notices to Airmen) is a critical skill for pilots, ensuring they are aware of temporary changes affecting the National Airspace System (NAS) that could impact flight safety and operations. NOTAMs provide timely information about conditions such as construction, natural phenomena, and other temporary changes not known in time to be published in the Aeronautical Information Publication (AIP). Pilots must check for relevant NOTAMs as part of their pre-flight planning process to ensure the safety and legality of their flight operations. The Federal Aviation Administration (FAA) categorizes NOTAMs into several types, including NOTAM (D) for information requiring wide dissemination, FDC NOTAMs for regulatory information, and Pointer NOTAMs that highlight or point to other important NOTAMs. Pilots can access NOTAMs through various means, including the FAA's NOTAM Search tool, flight service stations, or other approved third-party providers. When interpreting NOTAMs, it is essential for pilots to understand the specific terminology and abbreviations used, as these can significantly impact the interpretation and applicability of the information provided. For example, terms such as "RWY" for runway or "TWY" for taxiway are commonly used abbreviations in NOTAMs. Pilots should also be aware of the effective times and dates of NOTAMs, as these indicate when the NOTAMs become active and when they expire, which is crucial for flight planning purposes.

Calculating Weight and Balance is another fundamental exercise that ensures the aircraft operates within its performance limitations. Proper weight and balance calculation is not only a regulatory requirement but also a critical factor for safe flight operations. Pilots must determine the loaded weight of the aircraft and ensure it does not exceed the manufacturer's specified maximum takeoff weight. Additionally, the distribution of this weight must be such that the center of gravity (CG) falls within the allowable limits. To calculate weight and balance, pilots use the basic formula: Weight x Arm = Moment. The "arm" is the distance from a reference datum line, which is an imaginary vertical plane from which all horizontal distances are measured for balance purposes. By summing the moments and dividing by the total weight, pilots can determine the aircraft's CG and verify that it is within the allowable range. This calculation is crucial for different phases of flight, including takeoff, cruising, and landing, as an improperly balanced aircraft can significantly affect its handling characteristics and overall performance.

Reading and Interpreting METARs and TAFs are skills that enable pilots to understand current and forecasted weather conditions, respectively. METARs provide a snapshot of the weather conditions at an airport at a specific time, including information on wind, visibility, sky condition, temperature, dew point, and barometric pressure. TAFs, on the other hand, offer forecasts for a specific airport, covering a 24-hour period and providing details on expected changes in weather elements such as wind, visibility, and sky condition. Pilots must be proficient in decoding the abbreviations and codes used in METARs and TAFs to accurately assess weather conditions for flight planning and decision-making. For example, understanding that "BKN" stands for "broken clouds" and "10SM" indicates a visibility of 10 statute miles is essential for interpreting these reports. This proficiency ensures pilots can make informed decisions regarding flight routes, altitudes, and the need for alternate plans due to weather conditions.

Planning a Cross-Country Flight under VFR requires pilots to apply their knowledge of airspace, weather, navigation, and aircraft performance to ensure a safe and efficient flight. This exercise involves selecting a route that considers terrain, airspace restrictions, and available airports for refueling or emergency landings. Pilots must also calculate fuel requirements, considering factors such as wind, aircraft weight, and cruise speed to ensure they have sufficient fuel reserves as required by regulations. Additionally, pilots must prepare for potential weather changes by identifying alternate airports and incorporating them into their flight plan. This comprehensive planning process is crucial for mitigating risks and ensuring the safety of cross-country flights under visual flight rules.

Planning a Cross-Country Flight under IFR introduces additional considerations, such as filing an IFR flight plan, understanding instrument approach procedures, and navigating through controlled airspace. Pilots must be proficient in reading and interpreting instrument approach plates, which provide detailed information on how to safely approach and land at an airport under instrument conditions. This includes understanding minimum altitudes, missed approach procedures, and navigation aids used for the approach. Pilots must also be familiar with air traffic control (ATC) procedures for IFR flights, including how to communicate effectively with ATC and comply with clearances and instructions. This planning process ensures pilots can safely conduct flights under instrument flight rules, navigating through various weather conditions and airspace configurations.

Aircraft Performance Charts and Calculations are indispensable tools for pilots to ensure that their aircraft operates within safe parameters for every flight. These charts provide critical data on takeoff, landing distances, rate of climb, and cruise speed under various conditions such as weight, altitude, and temperature. Pilots must adeptly interpret these charts to make informed decisions about their flight plan, particularly when operating from airports with short runways or in high-density altitudes where aircraft performance can be significantly impacted. Mastery of these calculations allows for precise planning and adjustments to flight operations, enhancing safety and efficiency.

Emergency Procedure Simulation exercises are vital for preparing pilots to handle unforeseen events during flight effectively. These simulations cover a range of scenarios, including engine failures, electrical system malfunctions, and in-flight fire management. By practicing these procedures in a simulated environment, pilots can develop the muscle memory and decision-making skills necessary to respond calmly and correctly under pressure. This preparation is crucial for ensuring that pilots can maintain control of the aircraft and navigate safely to an appropriate landing area or resolve the issue in flight, thereby safeguarding the lives of everyone on board.

Radio Communication Scenarios are designed to enhance pilots' proficiency in using aviation radio communications effectively. These exercises simulate interactions with air traffic control (ATC), including clearances for takeoff and landing, requests for altitude changes, and how to communicate in emergency situations. Effective radio communication is essential for maintaining situational awareness and ensuring compliance with ATC instructions, which are critical for the safe and orderly flow of air traffic within controlled airspace. Pilots must be adept at both understanding and conveying information clearly and succinctly, using standard aviation phraseology to minimize misunderstandings.

Navigational Aids Usage focuses on teaching pilots how to utilize various navigational tools and systems, such as VORs (VHF Omnidirectional Range), GPS (Global Positioning System), and ADFs (Automatic Direction Finders). These aids are essential for determining the aircraft's position and navigating along a flight path, especially under instrument flight rules (IFR) or in poor visibility conditions. Exercises include plotting courses, interpreting navigational signals, and using electronic flight instruments to maintain situational awareness. Proficiency in these areas is crucial for ensuring that pilots can navigate accurately and efficiently, reducing the risk of deviations from the intended flight path.

Decision Making in Emergency Situations drills into the critical thinking and rapid decision-making skills needed when confronted with an in-flight emergency. Pilots are presented with scenarios that require immediate assessment, prioritization of actions, and implementation of the best course of action to mitigate the situation. These exercises reinforce the importance of maintaining composure, utilizing available resources, and executing emergency procedures as trained. The goal is to ensure that pilots are prepared to make informed decisions that maximize the safety of flight operations under adverse conditions.

Identifying and Responding to Airspace Infringements is an exercise that focuses on preventing unauthorized entry into restricted or controlled airspace. Pilots are trained to recognize the boundaries of different airspace types and understand the requirements for entry, including communication with ATC and adherence to specific flight rules. This training is essential for avoiding potential conflicts with other aircraft and ensuring compliance with federal aviation regulations, thereby maintaining the safety and security of the airspace system.

Understanding and Applying Weather Information teaches pilots how to interpret and use weather data to make informed decisions about flight operations. This includes understanding weather patterns, fronts, and systems, as well as interpreting forecasts and real-time weather updates. Pilots learn to assess the impact of weather on flight safety, including considerations for turbulence, icing conditions, and visibility. This knowledge is critical for planning safe flight routes, making go/no-go decisions, and adjusting plans as necessary in response to changing weather conditions.

Pre-flight Inspection Procedures ensure that pilots are thoroughly familiar with the steps required to assess the airworthiness of their aircraft before takeoff. This includes checking the condition of the aircraft's structure, control systems, propulsion system, and avionics, as well as verifying that all necessary documentation is on board. These inspections are crucial for identifying any issues that could affect the safety of the flight, ensuring that the aircraft is in proper working order before departure.

Fuel Planning and Management exercises teach pilots how to calculate fuel requirements for a flight, taking into consideration factors such as distance, winds, aircraft weight, and reserves required by regulations. Pilots learn strategies for monitoring fuel consumption during flight and making adjustments as necessary to ensure that they always have sufficient fuel to reach their destination or an alternate airport if needed. This training is essential for preventing fuel starvation situations and ensuring safe flight operations.

Understanding and Interpreting Air Traffic Control Instructions is designed to ensure that pilots can accurately comprehend and follow the directives issued by ATC. This includes understanding clearances for takeoff and landing, route modifications, and instructions for altitude or speed adjustments. Mastery of this skill is essential for maintaining separation from other aircraft and navigating safely through controlled airspace, contributing to the overall safety and efficiency of the National Airspace System.

Simulated Instrument Flight Rules (IFR) Flight and Simulated Visual Flight Rules (VFR) Flight exercises provide pilots with the opportunity to apply their knowledge and skills in a controlled, simulated environment. These exercises cover everything from flight planning and navigation to communication with ATC and adherence to flight rules. The goal is to ensure that pilots are well-prepared to conduct both VFR and IFR flights in real-world conditions, enhancing their competence and confidence in the

Understanding NOTAMs

Question: What is the primary purpose of a NOTAM (Notice to Airmen)?

- A) To inform pilots of temporary changes to the National Airspace System (NAS) that are not known far enough in advance to be published in the Aeronautical Information Publication (AIP).
- B) To provide pilots with updates on permanent changes to the NAS.
- C) To notify pilots about airshows and other aviation-related events.

Correct answer explanation: A) To inform pilots of temporary changes to the National Airspace System (NAS) that are not known far enough in advance to be published in the Aeronautical Information Publication (AIP).

NOTAMs are issued to alert aircraft pilots of potential hazards along a flight route or at a location that could affect the flight's safety. These notices are critical for pre-flight planning and are issued to communicate information such as temporary changes to the NAS, including but not limited to, construction activities, air traffic services and facilities changes, or conditions at an aerodrome, like runway closures or lighting outages. Unlike permanent changes, which are incorporated into the AIP and other navigational publications on a regular schedule, NOTAMs address the need for timely dissemination of essential operational information that could impact flight safety. Understanding and adhering to the information conveyed through NOTAMs is a fundamental responsibility of all pilots to ensure the safety of flight operations.

Calculating Weight and Balance

Question: You are planning a cross-country flight in a Cessna 172. The aircraft's basic empty weight is 1,600 pounds, and the basic empty weight moment is 64,000 inch-pounds. You will have a pilot and one passenger, with a combined weight of 330 pounds, and you plan to carry 100 pounds of baggage. The aircraft will be fully fueled with 40 gallons of avgas, with each gallon weighing 6 pounds. Calculate the aircraft's total weight and determine if it is within the Cessna 172's maximum allowable takeoff weight of 2,450 pounds. Additionally,

calculate the aircraft's center of gravity (CG) and verify if it falls within the allowable CG range of 35 to 47.3 inches.

- A) Total Weight: 2,430 pounds, CG: 42 inches; within limits.
- B) Total Weight: 2,470 pounds, CG: 46 inches; exceeds maximum takeoff weight.
- C) Total Weight: 2,410 pounds, CG: 44 inches; within limits.

Correct answer explanation: A) Total Weight: 2,430 pounds, CG: 42 inches; within limits.

Problem description

To calculate the total weight, add the basic empty weight of the aircraft (1,600 pounds) to the weight of the pilot and passenger (330 pounds), the weight of the baggage (100 pounds), and the weight of the fuel. The fuel weight is calculated by multiplying the number of gallons (40) by the weight of one gallon of avgas (6 pounds), which equals 240 pounds.

Total weight = 1,600 + 330 + 100 + 240 = 2,270 pounds.

To calculate the aircraft's center of gravity (CG), first calculate the moment of each component (weight multiplied by arm). The arm is the distance from the reference datum to the center of gravity of an item. Assuming standard arms for the pilot and passenger, baggage, and fuel, calculate each moment, then divide the total moment by the total weight to find the CG.

Assuming arms (not provided, but necessary for calculation in real scenarios) are as follows:
- Pilot and passenger: 37 inches
- Baggage: 95 inches
- Fuel: 48 inches

Calculate moments:
- Pilot and passenger moment = 330 pounds * 37 inches = 12,210 inch-pounds
- Baggage moment = 100 pounds * 95 inches = 9,500 inch-pounds
- Fuel moment = 240 pounds * 48 inches = 11,520 inch-pounds

Total moment = Basic empty weight moment + Pilot and passenger moment + Baggage moment + Fuel moment
Total moment = 64,000 + 12,210 + 9,500 + 11,520 = 97,230 inch-pounds

To find the CG, divide the total moment by the total weight:
CG = Total moment / Total weight = 97,230 inch-pounds / 2,270 pounds = 42.8 inches

Since the total weight of 2,270 pounds is less than the maximum allowable takeoff weight of 2,450 pounds and the CG of 42.8 inches falls within the allowable CG range of 35 to 47.3 inches, the aircraft is within limits for safe flight.

Note: The initial total weight calculation provided in the question was incorrect, leading to an adjusted explanation to align with the correct calculation methodology.

Reading and Interpreting METARs and TAFs

Question: Decode the following METAR report for John F. Kennedy International Airport (JFK): "KJFK 121651Z 18015G25KT 10SM FEW020 SCT250 30/22 A2992 RMK AO2 SLP134 T03000220."

- A) At JFK, on the 12th at 1651Z, winds are from the south at 15 knots, gusting to 25 knots. Visibility is 10 statute miles with a few clouds at 2,000 feet and scattered clouds at 25,000 feet. The temperature is 30°C with a dew point of 22°C. The altimeter setting is 29.92 inches of mercury. Remarks: Automated observation with precipitation discriminator, sea-level pressure is 1013.4 mb, and the temperature is 30.0°C with a dew point of 22.0°C.
- B) At JFK, on the 12th at 1651Z, winds are from the south at 180 degrees at 15 knots. Visibility is 10 statute miles with a few clouds at 20,000 feet and scattered clouds at 2,500 feet. The temperature is 22°C with a dew point of 30°C. The altimeter setting is 29.92 inches of mercury. Remarks: Manual observation without precipitation discriminator, sea-level pressure is 1134 mb, and the temperature is 22.0°C with a dew point of 30.0°C.
- C) At JFK, on the 12th at 1651Z, winds are from the south at 180 degrees at 15 knots, gusting to 25 knots. Visibility is 10 statute miles with a few

clouds at 2,000 feet and scattered clouds at 25,000 feet. The temperature is 30°C with a dew point of 22°C. The altimeter setting is 29.92 inches of mercury. Remarks: Automated observation without precipitation discriminator, sea-level pressure is 1134 mb, and the temperature is 22.0°C with a dew point of 30.0°C.

Correct answer explanation: A) At JFK, on the 12th at 1651Z, winds are from the south at 15 knots, gusting to 25 knots. Visibility is 10 statute miles with a few clouds at 2,000 feet and scattered clouds at 25,000 feet. The temperature is 30°C with a dew point of 22°C. The altimeter setting is 29.92 inches of mercury. Remarks: Automated observation with precipitation discriminator, sea-level pressure is 1013.4 mb, and the temperature is 30.0°C with a dew point of 22.0°C.

Problem description

To decode this METAR, one must understand each segment of the report:
- **KJFK** indicates the station identifier for John F. Kennedy International Airport.
- **121651Z** shows the date and time of the report, which is the 12th of the month at 1651Z (Zulu time).
- **18015G25KT** describes the wind direction and speed, coming from 180 degrees at 15 knots, gusting to 25 knots.
- **10SM** indicates the visibility is 10 statute miles.
- **FEW020 SCT250** describes the cloud cover, with few clouds at 2,000 feet and scattered clouds at 25,000 feet.
- **30/22** provides the temperature and dew point in Celsius, 30°C and 22°C respectively.
- **A2992** is the altimeter setting, 29.92 inches of mercury.
- **RMK AO2 SLP134 T03000220** in the remarks section, "AO2" indicates an automated station with a precipitation discriminator, "SLP134" translates to a sea-level pressure of 1013.4 mb, and "T03000220" confirms the temperature and dew point.

Solution explanation

By breaking down each component of the METAR report, one can accurately interpret the current weather conditions at JFK Airport. The correct answer is A) because it correctly decodes the wind direction and speed, visibility, cloud cover, temperature, dew point, altimeter setting, and includes the correct interpretation of the remarks section.

Understanding how to read METAR reports is crucial for pilots and aviation professionals to assess weather conditions accurately.

Planning a Cross-Country Flight under VFR

Problem description

You are tasked with planning a cross-country flight under Visual Flight Rules (VFR) from John F. Kennedy International Airport (JFK) in New York to Miami International Airport (MIA) in Florida. Your aircraft is a Piper PA-28 Cherokee with a cruise speed of 110 knots and a fuel capacity that allows for 4.5 hours of flight time at cruise speed, with a 45-minute reserve.

1. Determine the total distance of the flight and compare it to the aircraft's range to ensure the flight can be completed with at least one refueling stop.
2. Identify a suitable airport for refueling, considering the halfway point of your journey and the availability of fuel services.
3. Calculate the total estimated flight time, including a 15-minute buffer for takeoff and landing at each airport.
4. Plan for altitude, taking into account the terrain and airspace you will encounter along the route.
5. Prepare a flight log that includes waypoints, frequencies for navigation aids (NAVAIDs), and estimated times over each waypoint.
6. Consider weather forecasts and NOTAMs for your departure, en route, and arrival times to adjust your flight plan as necessary.

Solution explanation

1. The total distance from JFK to MIA is approximately 1,090 nautical miles. Given the PA-28's range of approximately 495 nautical miles (110 knots * 4.5 hours), you will need to plan for at least two refueling stops.

2. A suitable airport for refueling is Raleigh-Durham International Airport (RDU) in North Carolina, approximately 425 nautical miles from JFK, and Orlando Executive Airport (ORL) in Florida, approximately 600 nautical

miles from RDU. Both airports offer full-service fueling options and are conveniently located along the route.

3. The total estimated flight time from JFK to MIA, including refueling stops, is approximately 10 hours and 30 minutes. This estimate includes 9 hours of flight time (1,090 NM / 110 knots) and 1.5 hours for refueling and buffer time.

4. An altitude of 7,500 feet for the majority of the flight is recommended to ensure a safe clearance above terrain and to optimize fuel efficiency. Adjustments may be necessary for airspace transitions, particularly when approaching and departing from major airports.

5. The flight log should include waypoints such as VOR stations and intersections along the route, with frequencies and estimated times noted. For example, JFK VOR (115.9 MHz) departure, SWL (113.5 MHz) over the Delmarva Peninsula, RDU VOR (117.2 MHz) for the first refueling stop, and so on, until reaching MIA.

6. Weather forecasts indicate VFR conditions for the majority of the route, with some scattered clouds at 5,000 feet near the Florida coast. NOTAMs include a temporary flight restriction (TFR) near Washington, D.C., requiring a slight route adjustment to the west. Additionally, runway maintenance at ORL will necessitate using an alternate runway for your refueling stop.

By carefully planning the flight with attention to distance, refueling stops, flight time, altitude, navigation, and adjusting for weather and NOTAMs, you can ensure a safe and efficient cross-country flight under VFR from JFK to MIA.

Planning a Cross-Country Flight under IFR

Problem description

You are planning a cross-country flight under Instrument Flight Rules (IFR) from Chicago O'Hare International Airport (ORD) to Los Angeles International Airport (LAX). Your aircraft is a Beechcraft Baron 58, which has a cruising speed of 200 knots and a range of 1,500 nautical miles with reserves.

1. Calculate the total distance of the flight plan and verify it is within the aircraft's range, considering required IFR reserves.
2. Select appropriate IFR waypoints and navigational aids (NAVAIDs) to outline your route, ensuring compliance with air traffic control (ATC) requirements for altitude and route structure.
3. Determine the total estimated flight time, factoring in average headwinds of 20 knots.
4. Plan for an alternate airport, considering forecasted weather conditions at LAX and IFR alternate airport requirements.
5. Create a fuel plan, including takeoff, en route burn, and reserves as per IFR regulations.
6. Evaluate NOTAMs and TFRs (Temporary Flight Restrictions) that could affect your flight plan and make necessary adjustments.

Solution explanation

1. The total distance from ORD to LAX, following a typical IFR route, is approximately 1,750 nautical miles. Given the Beechcraft Baron 58's range of 1,500 nautical miles with reserves, the flight is within the aircraft's capabilities, but careful fuel management and planning for an en route fuel stop are necessary. A suitable fuel stop could be Albuquerque International Sunport (ABQ), roughly halfway and a common stop for cross-country flights.

2. Utilizing the FAA's preferred IFR routes and considering altitude and route structure requirements, a plausible routing could be ORD to DBQ (Dubuque VOR), then ONL (O'Neill VORTAC), followed by SNY (Sidney VOR), then JNC (Grand Junction VOR), and finally LAX. This route takes advantage of major VORs and ensures compliance with ATC's altitude assignments and route structures for cross-country IFR flight.

3. Considering the cruising speed of 200 knots and accounting for an average headwind of 20 knots, the estimated flight time from ORD to LAX, including the stop at ABQ, would be approximately 9.5 hours. This estimate includes time for ascent, descent, and the approach at both the fuel stop and destination airport.

4. For an alternate airport, Bob Hope Airport (BUR) in Burbank, CA, is a suitable choice given its proximity to LAX and the likelihood of meeting IFR alternate minimums, which require forecasted weather at the alternate to

be no worse than 600 feet ceiling and 2 statute miles visibility for precision approaches.

5. The fuel plan should include fuel for takeoff, climb, cruise, descent, and approach phases, plus a 45-minute reserve as required by IFR regulations. Additional fuel for the possibility of holding, deviations for weather, and routing to the alternate airport should also be factored in. Based on the Baron 58's fuel burn rate, planning for approximately 120 gallons of fuel for the main leg, 60 gallons for the leg to the alternate airport, and reserves would be prudent.

6. Reviewing NOTAMs and TFRs is crucial for identifying any airspace closures, restrictions, or changes in ATC procedures that could impact the flight. For example, a TFR over a major sporting event or VIP movement could necessitate a route adjustment. For this flight, ensuring no TFRs affect the planned route or stops, especially in major metropolitan areas like Chicago and Los Angeles, is essential. Adjustments to the flight plan may include rerouting or timing adjustments to avoid active TFR periods.

By meticulously planning the route, fuel stops, and considering all regulatory requirements and potential weather and airspace restrictions, the flight from ORD to LAX under IFR can be conducted safely and efficiently.

Aircraft Performance Charts and Calculations

Problem description

You are tasked with planning a flight for a Piper PA-28 Cherokee from San Francisco International Airport (SFO) to Las Vegas McCarran International Airport (LAS). The aircraft's performance charts indicate a fuel consumption rate of 8.4 gallons per hour at a cruising speed of 120 knots. The total distance between SFO and LAS is approximately 414 nautical miles. You need to calculate the total estimated flight time, considering an additional 10% of the flight time as a reserve, and determine the total amount of fuel required for the trip, including the reserve. The aircraft's maximum fuel capacity is 48 gallons. Assess whether the planned flight is feasible with the available fuel capacity.

Solution explanation

First, calculate the estimated flight time without reserve:

- Flight time = Total distance / Cruising speed = 414 NM / 120 knots ≈ 3.45 hours

Next, calculate the 10% reserve time:

- Reserve time = Flight time * 10% = 3.45 hours * 0.1 = 0.345 hours

Add the reserve time to the initial flight time to get the total estimated flight time:

- Total flight time with reserve = 3.45 hours + 0.345 hours ≈ 3.8 hours

Now, calculate the total amount of fuel required:

- Total fuel required = Total flight time with reserve * Fuel consumption rate = 3.8 hours * 8.4 gallons/hour ≈ 31.92 gallons

Finally, assess the feasibility of the flight based on the aircraft's maximum fuel capacity:

- Since the total fuel required (31.92 gallons) is less than the aircraft's maximum fuel capacity (48 gallons), the planned flight is feasible with the available fuel capacity.

Emergency Procedure Simulation

Problem description

You are flying a Piper PA-28 Cherokee on a cross-country flight when you encounter unexpected severe weather. The aircraft begins to experience heavy turbulence and a significant decrease in engine power. You suspect carburetor icing and need to navigate to the nearest airport for an emergency landing. The nearest airport is 25 nautical miles away, directly north. You must manage the aircraft's altitude, airspeed, and heading to ensure a safe approach and landing, considering the following:

1. Implement the carburetor heat as per the emergency procedures to mitigate the icing.
2. Adjust the mixture for optimal performance in the current weather conditions.
3. Communicate with ATC to declare an emergency and receive immediate clearance and assistance.
4. Navigate towards the nearest airport using VOR navigation, maintaining visual contact with the ground as much as possible.
5. Prepare for an emergency landing, including briefing any passengers, securing loose items, and reviewing the landing checklist.

Solution explanation

1. Immediately apply full carburetor heat to melt any ice that has formed. This action should be taken without hesitation as carburetor icing can lead to a complete engine failure if not addressed promptly.

2. Adjust the mixture control to enrich the fuel mixture, which can help improve engine performance in cold, moist conditions where carburetor icing is a risk. However, be mindful of the altitude and the engine's response to these adjustments.

3. Declare an emergency with ATC by stating "Mayday, Mayday, Mayday," followed by your aircraft identification, nature of the emergency, intention (to land at the nearest airport), and request for immediate assistance. This will ensure you receive priority handling by ATC, clearing the airspace and providing any necessary guidance to the nearest airport.

4. Use the VOR navigation to set a direct course to the nearest airport. If VOR is not available or you are unable to navigate due to the situation, follow ATC instructions for heading and altitude adjustments to reach the airport safely. Keep visual contact with the ground if possible to maintain spatial orientation and avoid controlled flight into terrain.

5. Brief any passengers on the emergency procedures, including brace positions and the location of emergency exits. Secure any loose items in the cabin to prevent injury during turbulence or the landing. Review the emergency landing checklist, ensuring that seat belts are fastened, fuel supply is set to the fullest tank, landing lights are on if visibility is poor, and flaps are set as required for an emergency landing.

By methodically addressing each step, you can manage the emergency situation, mitigate risks, and safely navigate to an emergency landing at the nearest airport.

Radio Communication Scenarios

Problem description

You are piloting a Cessna 172 on a cross-country flight under VFR conditions. Halfway through your flight, you realize you need to divert to a nearby airport due to unexpected weather conditions. You decide to divert to Springfield Airport, which is unfamiliar to you. You need to establish radio communication with Springfield Tower to request permission to land, obtain the current weather conditions, and understand any specific landing instructions or advisories that might affect your approach and landing.

1. Tune your radio to the frequency for Springfield Tower.
2. Properly announce your aircraft, position, altitude, and intentions to Springfield Tower.
3. Request the current weather conditions at Springfield Airport.
4. Ask for any special advisories or instructions for landing.

Solution explanation

1. First, locate the frequency for Springfield Tower from your sectional chart or electronic flight bag (EFB) application. The frequency is 118.45 MHz. Tune your aircraft's radio to 118.45 MHz to establish communication.

2. Begin your communication with Springfield Tower by stating the tower's name, followed by your aircraft's identification, your current position relative to the airport, your altitude, and your intentions. For example, "Springfield Tower, Cessna 172, November 12345, 10 miles west at 3,500 feet, inbound for landing, with information Alpha."

3. After establishing communication and receiving acknowledgment from Springfield Tower, request the current weather conditions by saying, "Request current weather at Springfield Airport."

4. Finally, inquire about any special advisories or instructions that might affect your approach and landing by asking, "Are there any special advisories or landing instructions for Cessna November 12345?"

By following these steps, you ensure clear and effective communication with Springfield Tower, which is essential for a safe diversion and landing at an unfamiliar airport. Proper radio communication helps maintain situational awareness and ensures compliance with air traffic control instructions and advisories.

Navigational Aids Usage

Problem description

You are planning an IFR flight from Denver International Airport (DEN) to Seattle-Tacoma International Airport (SEA). Your aircraft is equipped with standard navigation aids including VOR, DME, and GPS. You need to select the most efficient route using these navigational aids while ensuring compliance with FAA regulations and considering terrain and airspace restrictions. Your tasks include:

1. Identify the primary VORs along the route that you will use for navigation.
2. Calculate the total distance using the selected VORs.
3. Plan for altitude changes required by airspace restrictions and terrain.
4. Determine the estimated time en route (ETE) considering an average groundspeed of 250 knots.
5. Adjust your flight plan for a known Temporary Flight Restriction (TFR) over the central Rocky Mountains.

Solution explanation

1. The primary VORs for this route could include Cheyenne (CYS), Rock Springs (RKS), and Boise (BOI). These VORs are strategically located to guide the flight path from DEN to SEA efficiently while considering terrain and airspace restrictions.

2. The total distance using these VORs can be calculated by adding the segment distances: DEN to CYS (about 80 NM), CYS to RKS (about 230

NM), RKS to BOI (about 250 NM), and BOI to SEA (about 300 NM). This totals approximately 860 nautical miles.

3. Altitude planning must consider the elevation of the Rocky Mountains and Cascade Range. A cruising altitude of at least FL250 (25,000 feet) is recommended to ensure terrain clearance and compliance with airspace restrictions. However, adjustments may be necessary for the TFR and to optimize for wind conditions.

4. The estimated time en route (ETE) can be calculated by dividing the total distance by the average groundspeed. For 860 NM at 250 knots, the ETE is approximately 3.44 hours or about 3 hours and 26 minutes.

5. Given the TFR over the central Rocky Mountains, a slight detour to the north may be necessary. Adjusting the route to include a waypoint north of the TFR, such as passing near Salt Lake City (SLC) before heading to BOI, could add approximately 50 NM to the flight. This adjustment increases the total distance to about 910 NM and the ETE to approximately 3.64 hours or about 3 hours and 38 minutes.

By selecting appropriate VORs, calculating distances, planning for altitude, estimating time en route, and adjusting for airspace restrictions, you can efficiently and safely plan an IFR flight from DEN to SEA.

Decision Making in Emergency Situations

Problem description

While en route in a Cessna 172 for a cross-country flight under VFR conditions, you encounter a sudden and severe electrical failure. The aircraft's avionics shut down, leaving you without radio communication, navigation aids, or transponder capabilities. You are currently flying over mountainous terrain with the nearest airport, Mountain View Airport, approximately 30 nautical miles to the east. The weather is clear, but it's nearing sunset, and you are aware that navigating through the mountains during twilight could be hazardous without precise navigation aids. You need to make critical decisions to ensure a safe outcome.

1. Determine the immediate actions to take following the recognition of the electrical failure.

2. Devise a plan to navigate towards Mountain View Airport without the use of electronic navigation aids.
3. Prepare for the possibility of a communication failure with the airport's control tower.
4. Consider the steps to ensure a safe landing, given the limited visibility and lack of communication.

Solution explanation

1. Upon recognizing the electrical failure, the first action is to attempt to reset the electrical system by checking the circuit breakers and, if safe, resetting any that have popped. If this doesn't restore power, switch to the battery to see if there's any remaining power for critical systems. Simultaneously, maintain visual flight by keeping the aircraft stable and at a safe altitude, clear of terrain.

2. To navigate towards Mountain View Airport without electronic aids, use the emergency section of the VFR sectional chart, which you should have readily accessible. Identify prominent landmarks, such as highways, rivers, or mountain peaks, that can guide you to the airport. Since it's nearing sunset, also use the direction of the sun as a general guide eastward.

3. With the expectation of a communication failure, review the light gun signals in the Pilot's Operating Handbook (POH) or your pilot's kneeboard if available, as the control tower may use these to give you landing clearance. Also, remember the common traffic advisory frequency (CTAF) for Mountain View Airport might still be monitored by other pilots who can relay messages on your behalf if you can briefly restore power or use a handheld transceiver.

4. For a safe landing, especially with limited visibility and no communication, enter the traffic pattern at a 45-degree angle to the downwind leg if possible, to integrate with any other traffic visually. Keep the cockpit lights dim to enhance outside visibility during twilight. Perform a thorough pre-landing checklist by memory, including configuring the aircraft for landing (flaps, landing gear down) and ensuring you have selected the correct runway by observing the windsock for wind direction. Plan for a full-stop landing, avoiding any unnecessary maneuvers once on final approach.

By systematically addressing each step, you can manage the electrical failure emergency, navigate safely to Mountain View Airport, and prepare for landing under challenging conditions.

Identifying and Responding to Airspace Infringements

Problem description

You are piloting a Cessna 172 on a VFR cross-country flight. During the flight, you inadvertently enter a Restricted Area (RA) that is currently active for military use. You realize the mistake when ATC contacts you, advising you of the airspace infringement. You must quickly and safely exit the RA, communicate effectively with ATC, and ensure compliance with all regulations to mitigate the situation.

Solution explanation

1. **Immediately acknowledge ATC's communication**: Confirm receipt of the message and your current position, indicating that you are taking immediate action to exit the Restricted Area.

2. **Determine the quickest and safest route out of the RA**: Utilize your onboard navigation tools to identify your current location and the shortest path out of the RA. If possible, turn towards the direction from which you entered the RA to minimize your time within the restricted space.

3. **Communicate your exit plan to ATC**: Clearly inform ATC of your intended route out of the RA. This includes your heading, altitude adjustments if necessary, and estimated time to exit the RA. Request any additional instructions or information that could assist in safely resolving the situation.

4. **Adjust your heading and altitude as needed**: Based on your exit plan and any instructions from ATC, make the necessary changes to your heading and altitude to leave the RA as quickly and safely as possible.

5. **Review and comply with any potential follow-up actions**: After exiting the RA, ATC may provide instructions for follow-up actions, such as filing a

report or contacting a specific FAA office. Ensure to comply with these instructions promptly.

6. Reflect on the incident to prevent future airspace infringements: After completing your flight, review the circumstances that led to the airspace infringement. Identify any gaps in your pre-flight planning or in-flight navigation practices and take steps to address them. This might include additional training on airspace awareness or the use of navigation aids.

By taking immediate action to exit the Restricted Area, maintaining clear and concise communication with ATC, and complying with follow-up procedures, you can effectively manage the situation and minimize the impact of the airspace infringement.

Understanding and Applying Weather Information

Problem description

You are planning a VFR cross-country flight from San Diego International Airport (SAN) to San Francisco International Airport (SFO). The forecasted weather along your route includes areas of low visibility due to fog and mist in the early morning hours, with conditions improving by midday. Additionally, there are reports of scattered thunderstorms developing in the afternoon near your destination. You must plan your departure time, altitude, and route to mitigate the risks posed by the weather conditions while ensuring compliance with VFR flight rules.

Solution explanation

1. **Analyze the weather forecast**: Begin by reviewing the Terminal Aerodrome Forecasts (TAFs) for both SAN and SFO, as well as the Area Forecast (FA) for the regions you will be flying through. Pay special attention to the forecasted visibility, cloud ceilings, and the timing and location of the thunderstorms.

2. **Plan your departure time**: Given the forecasted fog and mist in the early morning, plan a departure time that allows for conditions to improve to

VFR minimums. A mid-morning departure should ensure better visibility and higher cloud ceilings, reducing the risk of encountering IFR conditions.

3. **Choose an appropriate altitude**: Select a cruising altitude that keeps you clear of terrain and obstacles while providing a buffer below the cloud base. This altitude should also offer more options for diversion, should the weather deteriorate en route.

4. **Route planning**: Plot a route that avoids the areas forecasted to have thunderstorms by using navigational aids and visual checkpoints. Consider planning your route to include airports where you can land and wait if the thunderstorms move into your path.

5. **Briefing and decision-making**: Before departure, obtain a full weather briefing from Flight Service to verify that the weather conditions are as forecasted and that no new weather advisories have been issued. Be prepared to delay your departure or choose an alternate route based on the latest information.

6. **In-flight weather monitoring**: Use onboard weather equipment, if available, and communicate with Flight Service and Air Traffic Control (ATC) to receive updates on weather conditions along your route. Be ready to adjust your altitude or route as needed to maintain VFR conditions.

By carefully planning your departure time, altitude, and route, and by staying informed about the weather conditions before and during your flight, you can safely navigate the challenges posed by fog, mist, and thunderstorms on a VFR cross-country flight.

Pre-flight Inspection Procedures

Problem description

You are preparing for a morning flight in a Piper PA-28 Cherokee from a small, non-towered airport. Given the critical importance of a thorough pre-flight inspection to ensure the safety and airworthiness of the aircraft, you are tasked with performing a comprehensive pre-flight check. Your inspection must cover all necessary components and systems as outlined in the aircraft's Pilot's Operating Handbook (POH) and comply with Federal Aviation Regulations (FARs).

1. Review the aircraft's documentation, including the airworthiness certificate, registration, owner's manual, and maintenance records, to ensure they are current and onboard.
2. Conduct a walk-around inspection of the aircraft's exterior, paying close attention to the condition of the airframe, control surfaces, and landing gear.
3. Check the engine compartment for any signs of leaks, wear, or damage, and verify the oil level is within acceptable limits.
4. Inspect the propeller for nicks, cracks, or any other damage that could compromise its integrity.
5. Ensure the fuel quantity matches the flight plan requirements and verify the quality of the fuel.
6. Test the aircraft's lights, avionics, and all electrical systems to confirm they are operational.
7. Verify that all necessary emergency equipment, including a first aid kit, fire extinguisher, and life vests (if flying over water), are onboard and in good condition.
8. Perform control system checks to ensure freedom of movement and correct operation of the ailerons, rudder, and elevator.
9. Check the cabin and cockpit for any loose items that could interfere with the operation of the controls or distract the pilot during flight.

Solution explanation

1. **Documentation Check**: The first step involves ensuring the aircraft's documentation is not only present but also up to date. This includes the airworthiness certificate, which must be displayed in the aircraft, and the registration, which must be current. The owner's manual (or POH) provides critical information on the aircraft's operation and limitations, while maintenance records confirm compliance with all required inspections and repairs, ensuring the aircraft meets safety standards.

2. **Exterior Inspection**: During the walk-around, inspecting the airframe for structural integrity, checking control surfaces for secure attachment and undamaged condition, and verifying the landing gear for proper inflation and absence of leaks are essential. This step is crucial for identifying any potential issues that could affect the aircraft's performance and safety.

3. **Engine Compartment**: Checking the engine compartment involves looking for oil leaks, belt wear, and general condition of the engine parts.

The oil level must be within the manufacturer's recommended range to ensure proper lubrication and cooling of the engine.

4. **Propeller Inspection**: The propeller must be free of significant nicks, cracks, or bends. Even minor damage can lead to catastrophic failure due to the high forces exerted on the propeller during operation.

5. **Fuel Check**: Verifying the fuel quantity involves ensuring that the aircraft has enough fuel for the intended flight, plus reserves. Testing fuel quality, such as checking for water contamination or debris, is critical for engine performance and safety.

6. **Electrical Systems and Lights**: Testing all lights (navigation, strobe, landing) and electrical systems, including avionics, confirms their operational status. This step is vital for both daytime and nighttime operations, affecting communication, navigation, and visibility.

7. **Emergency Equipment**: Ensuring the presence and condition of emergency equipment is a regulatory requirement and a critical safety measure. This includes checking the expiration dates on first aid kits and fire extinguishers, and ensuring life vests are available for flights over water.

8. **Control System Check**: Moving the control surfaces through their full range of motion ensures there are no obstructions or malfunctions. This check confirms the aircraft's responsiveness to pilot inputs.

9. **Cabin and Cockpit Inspection**: Securing loose items prevents them from moving during flight, which could distract the pilot or interfere with the aircraft's controls. This step also includes ensuring the visibility and condition of all instruments and gauges.

By meticulously following these steps, a pilot ensures that the aircraft is in a condition for safe operation, complying with both the manufacturer's guidelines and federal regulations. This comprehensive pre-flight inspection is a fundamental part of flight preparation, significantly contributing to the safety of the flight.

Fuel Planning and Management

Problem description

You are planning a cross-country flight in a Piper PA-28 Cherokee from Los Angeles International Airport (LAX) to Chicago O'Hare International Airport (ORD). Your aircraft burns fuel at an average rate of 8.5 gallons per hour (GPH) under cruise conditions. The total distance of the flight is approximately 1,750 nautical miles (NM). Given the aircraft's fuel capacity is 48 gallons, calculate the number of required fuel stops assuming optimal conditions and no reserve fuel. Additionally, plan the locations for these stops considering major airports along the route and calculate the total fuel required for the trip including a 45-minute reserve as mandated by Federal Aviation Regulations for VFR day flights.

Solution explanation

1. **Calculate Total Flight Time**: First, determine the total flight time by dividing the total distance by the average speed. Assuming an average speed of 120 knots, the total flight time is 1,750 NM / 120 knots = 14.58 hours.

2. **Calculate Total Fuel Consumption Without Reserve**: Multiply the total flight time by the fuel burn rate to find out how much fuel is needed for the trip without reserves. 14.58 hours * 8.5 GPH = 124 gallons.

3. **Calculate Required Reserve Fuel**: Federal Aviation Regulations require a 45-minute reserve for VFR day flights. Calculate the reserve fuel as follows: 0.75 hours * 8.5 GPH = 6.375 gallons. For simplicity, round this to 6.4 gallons.

4. **Calculate Total Fuel Requirement Including Reserve**: Add the reserve fuel to the total fuel consumption calculated in step 2. 124 gallons + 6.4 gallons = 130.4 gallons.

5. **Determine Number of Fuel Stops**: Since the aircraft can carry 48 gallons, but the total fuel requirement is 130.4 gallons, divide the total requirement by the capacity to find the number of stops. 130.4 gallons / 48 gallons = 2.72. This means at least 3 fuel stops are required because you cannot partially fill for a fraction of a trip.

6. **Plan Fuel Stop Locations**: Considering major airports along the route and the aircraft's range, potential stops could include Albuquerque

International Sunport (ABQ), Kansas City International Airport (MCI), and Des Moines International Airport (DSM). Each segment between these stops is within the aircraft's range with a full fuel load.

7. **Recalculate Fuel Requirements with Stops**: With the stops planned, recalculate the fuel requirements for each leg to ensure accuracy, including taking off and climbing, which may increase fuel burn. This step might adjust the total fuel calculation slightly but ensures each leg is within the aircraft's fuel capacity.

By following these steps, you can efficiently plan the fuel management for a cross-country flight, ensuring compliance with regulations and safety through adequate reserves and well-planned refueling stops.

Understanding and Interpreting Air Traffic Control Instructions

Problem description

While flying under Instrument Flight Rules (IFR) in a Piper PA-28, you receive a rapid series of instructions from Air Traffic Control (ATC) due to unexpected severe weather conditions in your planned route. The instructions include an immediate altitude change, a heading adjustment to avoid the weather, and a frequency change for further communication. You must quickly interpret and respond to these instructions to ensure flight safety and compliance with ATC directives.

1. Identify the steps to correctly acknowledge and read back the ATC instructions.
2. Explain the procedure for changing altitude and heading in response to ATC instructions.
3. Describe the process for switching to a new communication frequency while maintaining situational awareness and flight safety.

Solution explanation

1. **Acknowledging ATC Instructions**: Upon receiving instructions from ATC, the first step is to listen carefully and write down the key points: altitude change, heading adjustment, and new frequency. Then, read back

the instructions to ATC to confirm understanding. This readback should include your call sign, the new altitude, the new heading, and the new frequency to ensure accuracy and compliance.

2. **Changing Altitude and Heading**: After acknowledging the instructions, begin the altitude change by adjusting the aircraft's vertical speed to a rate that is safe and appropriate for the current flight conditions. Simultaneously, adjust the heading using the aircraft's heading indicator or autopilot system, if equipped, to the new course directed by ATC. Monitor the altimeter and heading indicator closely to ensure adherence to the ATC instructions.

3. **Switching Communication Frequency**: Before changing the frequency, ensure that the aircraft is stable and that you have a clear understanding of the current and next steps in your flight plan. Switch the radio to the new frequency provided by ATC, but do not immediately transmit. Listen for a few seconds to ensure the frequency is not in use and to gain situational awareness of any relevant communications. Once clear, check in with the new ATC unit by stating your aircraft's call sign, current altitude, and that you have switched as instructed.

By following these steps, you maintain compliance with ATC instructions, ensuring both the safety of your flight and the efficiency of the airspace around you.

Simulated Instrument Flight Rules (IFR) Flight

Problem description

You are the pilot of a Beechcraft Baron flying under Instrument Flight Rules (IFR) from Chicago O'Hare International Airport (ORD) to Denver International Airport (DEN). Halfway through the flight, you encounter unexpected severe icing conditions not forecasted in the pre-flight weather briefing. The aircraft's de-icing systems are functioning, but the severity of the icing threatens to overwhelm the aircraft's capabilities. You must quickly decide on a course of action that ensures the safety of the flight while adhering to IFR regulations and procedures.

Solution explanation

1. **Assess the Situation**: Immediately assess the severity of the icing condition and the performance of the aircraft. Note any changes in airspeed, altitude, or control responsiveness.

2. **Communicate with ATC**: Without delay, inform Air Traffic Control (ATC) of your situation. Include your current position, altitude, the nature of the emergency (severe icing), and any immediate needs or requests, such as a change in altitude or route to warmer temperatures or clear of cloud layers.

3. **Request Altitude Change**: If conditions permit and it is safe to do so, request an immediate altitude change from ATC to either climb above the cloud layer or descend to an altitude where temperatures are above freezing. Specify the requested altitude change is due to severe icing conditions.

4. **Activate De-icing Systems**: Ensure all aircraft de-icing and anti-icing systems are activated and functioning correctly. Monitor these systems continuously to assess their effectiveness in mitigating ice accumulation.

5. **Prepare for Diversion**: If the icing condition does not improve or if the aircraft's performance deteriorates, prepare to divert to the nearest suitable airport. Communicate this intention to ATC, requesting radar vectors to the diversion airport.

6. **Monitor Aircraft Performance**: Continuously monitor the aircraft's performance, paying close attention to airspeed, altitude, engine power settings, and control responsiveness. Adjust as necessary to maintain safe flight conditions.

7. **Execute Diversion or Continue Flight**: Based on ATC instructions, the aircraft's performance, and the severity of the icing condition, make a decision to either continue to the original destination (if conditions improve) or divert to a safer location. If diverting, follow ATC instructions for the diversion and prepare for approach and landing.

8. **Document the Incident**: After landing safely, document the incident in detail, including the encountered conditions, actions taken, and any deviations from standard procedure. Report the incident to the appropriate aviation authorities as required.

By promptly assessing the situation, communicating effectively with ATC, and taking decisive action, you can navigate through unexpected severe icing conditions safely. This scenario emphasizes the importance of situational awareness, clear communication, and quick decision-making under IFR conditions.

Simulated Visual Flight Rules (VFR) Flight

Problem description

You are tasked with planning and executing a simulated Visual Flight Rules (VFR) flight from Asheville Regional Airport (AVL) to Raleigh-Durham International Airport (RDU) in a Cessna 172. The forecast predicts clear skies and light winds along the route, with a temporary weather system moving in that could bring cloud cover and reduced visibility to the destination airport by the afternoon. Your mission includes planning the route, calculating fuel requirements, and making in-flight decisions to ensure a safe and efficient flight under VFR conditions.

Solution explanation

1. **Route Planning**: Begin by charting the most direct route while considering airspace restrictions, terrain, and available navigation aids. Utilize VFR sectional charts to identify visual landmarks and checkpoints along the way. Plan to fly at an altitude that complies with VFR cruising altitude rules (odd thousand feet plus 500 feet when flying eastbound).

2. **Fuel Calculation**: Calculate the total fuel required based on the Cessna 172's average fuel consumption rate of 8.5 gallons per hour at cruise settings. Considering the distance is approximately 220 nautical miles and the average speed is 110 knots, the estimated flight time is 2 hours. With a 30-minute reserve required for VFR flights, calculate the total fuel needed for the trip.

3. **Weather Assessment**: Review the latest weather forecasts, Temporary Flight Restrictions (TFRs), and NOTAMs for the route and destination. Given the forecasted temporary weather system, plan for an early departure to avoid the incoming cloud cover and reduced visibility at RDU.

4. **Pre-flight Inspection**: Conduct a thorough pre-flight inspection of the aircraft, ensuring all systems are functional, and the aircraft is adequately fueled and equipped for the journey.

5. **In-flight Navigation**: Utilize pilotage and dead reckoning techniques to navigate, continuously verifying your position using visual landmarks and navigation aids. Stay alert to the changing weather conditions and be prepared to adjust your altitude or route as necessary to maintain VFR conditions.

6. **Communication**: Maintain regular communication with Air Traffic Control (ATC) and Flight Service Stations (FSS) for updates on weather and any airspace changes along your route. Use the appropriate radio frequencies as listed in the sectional chart and the Airport/Facility Directory.

7. **Decision Making for Weather**: If the weather at RDU begins to deteriorate before arrival, consider diverting to an alternate airport with better conditions. Use the information from the in-flight weather updates and ATC to make an informed decision.

8. **Landing Preparations**: As you approach RDU, obtain the latest ATIS information for the airport and prepare for the landing, considering the wind direction and speed for runway selection. Complete the pre-landing checklist, ensuring the aircraft configuration is appropriate for the approach and landing.

By following these steps, you will effectively plan and execute a VFR flight, demonstrating the ability to navigate using visual references, manage fuel, communicate with ATC, and make informed decisions in response to changing weather conditions.

Aircraft Systems Malfunction Procedures

Problem description

During a cross-country flight in a Cessna 172, you notice a sudden drop in oil pressure accompanied by an increase in engine temperature. You are currently flying over a rural area, with the nearest airport 25 nautical miles away. Given these symptoms, you must quickly diagnose the potential issue, decide on the best course of action to ensure the safety of the flight, and execute an emergency landing if necessary.

1. Identify the immediate steps to take upon noticing the drop in oil pressure and the increase in engine temperature.
2. Determine the potential causes of these symptoms and how they can affect the aircraft's performance.
3. Decide on the safest course of action, including whether to divert to the nearest airport or perform an emergency landing in a suitable area.
4. Outline the communication protocol with Air Traffic Control (ATC) during this emergency situation.

Solution explanation

1. **Immediate Steps**: Upon noticing a drop in oil pressure and an increase in engine temperature, immediately reduce power to minimize engine stress. Check the oil pressure gauge and engine temperature indicator for accurate readings. If equipped, use the aircraft's checklist for engine anomalies to guide your actions.

2. **Potential Causes and Effects**: The symptoms could indicate a serious engine issue, such as a leak in the oil system or an impending engine failure. A drop in oil pressure can lead to insufficient lubrication of engine components, causing overheating and potentially catastrophic engine damage.

3. **Safest Course of Action**: Given the rural setting and the distance to the nearest airport, assess the aircraft's ability to reach the airport safely. If the engine's condition worsens rapidly, prepare for an emergency landing in a suitable area, prioritizing open fields free of obstacles. If the engine remains stable, divert to the nearest airport, ensuring to plan the approach with consideration of the engine's uncertain reliability.

4. **Communication Protocol with ATC**: Immediately declare an emergency by stating "Mayday, Mayday, Mayday," followed by your aircraft identification, nature of the emergency, current position, and intentions. Follow ATC instructions, if able, and keep them informed of any changes in the aircraft's condition or your plans. If an off-airport landing becomes necessary, provide your best estimate of the landing site's location for emergency services.

By promptly recognizing the symptoms of an engine issue, assessing the situation, and taking decisive action, you can significantly increase the chances of a safe outcome in this emergency scenario. Communication with ATC and adherence to emergency procedures are crucial throughout the process.

Pilot's Bill of Rights in Practice

The Pilot's Bill of Rights (PBoR) serves as a cornerstone for aviators, ensuring fair treatment during investigations and enforcement actions by the Federal Aviation Administration (FAA) and the National Transportation Safety Board (NTSB). It is imperative for pilots to comprehend their rights and the procedural safeguards in place, which are designed to promote transparency and fairness. This understanding is not only crucial for legal compliance but also for maintaining the integrity and safety of aviation operations. Through practical scenarios, pilots can gain insights into the application of the PBoR, enhancing their ability to navigate the complexities of aviation law and regulation effectively.

Consider a scenario where a pilot is notified by the FAA of a potential violation of aviation regulations. The PBoR mandates that the pilot receives timely, written notification detailing the nature of the investigation. This ensures that the pilot is fully informed of the allegations and has a fair opportunity to respond. The scenario underscores the importance of understanding the notification process and the pilot's right to access investigative reports and evidence used by the FAA in the investigation. Pilots should be aware of their entitlement to obtain air traffic data, including voice recordings and radar information, which may be pivotal in their defense.

Another scenario involves a pilot undergoing an enforcement action. Here, the PBoR provides for the pilot's right to a fair trial, including the option to have the case heard by an administrative law judge at the NTSB. This scenario highlights the procedural aspects of challenging enforcement actions, emphasizing the pilot's ability to present evidence, call witnesses, and cross-examine FAA witnesses. It is crucial for pilots to recognize the significance of this judicial oversight mechanism in safeguarding their rights and interests.

Furthermore, the PBoR introduces protections related to the medical certification process for pilots. In scenarios where a pilot's medical certificate is under scrutiny, the PBoR ensures that the pilot receives specific information regarding the basis of the FAA's decision and the right to appeal that decision. This aspect of the PBoR is particularly relevant for pilots facing medical certification issues, as it provides a clear pathway to contest adverse decisions and seek a resolution.

In addition to these scenarios, the PBoR also addresses the importance of legal representation. Pilots have the right to be represented by an attorney or other representatives during FAA investigations and enforcement actions. This provision is critical in scenarios where the legal and regulatory complexities exceed the pilot's expertise. It ensures that pilots have access to professional guidance and support, leveling the playing field and enhancing the fairness of the process.

Through these practical scenarios, it becomes evident that the PBoR plays a vital role in protecting the rights of pilots within the regulatory framework of aviation. By familiarizing themselves with these rights and the procedures for asserting them, pilots can better navigate the challenges of investigations and enforcement actions. This knowledge not only contributes to individual legal protection but also promotes a culture of safety and accountability within the aviation community.

Chapter 15: Practical Exercises

To effectively navigate the complexities of aviation regulations and operational guidelines, it is essential for pilots and aviation professionals to engage in practical exercises that simulate real-world scenarios. These exercises are designed to reinforce understanding, enhance decision-making skills, and ensure preparedness for a variety of situations that may arise during flight operations. The following practical exercises focus on critical aspects of aviation safety, regulation compliance, and operational efficiency, providing a comprehensive training experience for participants.

One of the foundational exercises involves the interpretation and application of NOTAMs (Notice to Airmen). NOTAMs are crucial for the safety and efficiency of flight operations, providing timely information on airspace changes, temporary restrictions, and potential hazards. Participants will be tasked with analyzing a series of NOTAMs relevant to a planned flight route, identifying any that could impact the flight, and adjusting the flight plan accordingly. This exercise not only tests the ability to interpret NOTAMs accurately but also emphasizes the importance of flexibility and adaptability in flight planning.

Another critical exercise focuses on calculating weight and balance for an aircraft. Proper weight and balance are fundamental to ensuring aircraft performance and safety. Participants will be given a set of parameters, including aircraft specifications, passenger and cargo loads, and fuel requirements. Using this information, they will calculate the weight and balance to determine if the aircraft is within its allowable limits for safe operation. This exercise reinforces the mathematical and analytical skills necessary for effective flight planning and highlights the impact of weight and balance on aircraft performance.

Reading and interpreting METARs and TAFs (Meteorological Aerodrome Reports and Terminal Aerodrome Forecasts) is another essential skill that will be developed through practical exercises. Accurate weather interpretation is critical for safe flight operations, particularly under visual flight rules (VFR) and instrument flight rules (IFR). Participants will analyze current METARs and TAFs for specific airports, assess the impact of weather conditions on flight operations, and make informed decisions regarding flight go/no-go and necessary adjustments to flight plans. This exercise emphasizes the importance of weather awareness and the ability to integrate weather information into operational decision-making.

Planning a cross-country flight under VFR and IFR conditions will also be a key component of the practical exercises. Participants will be required to plan a flight from origin to destination, taking into consideration airspace classifications, air traffic control requirements, navigation aids, fuel requirements, alternate airports, and emergency procedures. This comprehensive exercise tests a wide range of skills, including route planning, navigation, regulatory compliance, and contingency planning, providing a holistic view of the complexities involved in flight planning and execution.

These practical exercises are designed to build upon the theoretical knowledge provided in the FAR/AIM 2025, applying it to realistic scenarios that aviation professionals may encounter. Through active engagement in these exercises, participants will develop a deeper understanding of federal aviation regulations, aeronautical information, and operational guidelines, enhancing their ability to operate safely and efficiently within the national airspace system.

To further enhance the practical understanding of aviation regulations and operational guidelines, additional exercises delve into the intricacies of aircraft performance charts and calculations. Participants will engage with real-world data, interpreting aircraft performance charts to make critical decisions regarding takeoff distances, climb rates, and fuel consumption under varying conditions. This exercise underscores the importance of precise calculations in ensuring the aircraft's optimal performance and safety throughout the flight.

Emergency procedure simulations form another crucial component of the training. Pilots and aviation professionals will be confronted with simulated emergency scenarios, ranging from engine failures to in-flight medical emergencies. The objective is to apply critical thinking and decision-making skills to navigate these situations effectively, utilizing the procedures outlined in the FAR/AIM. This exercise not only tests the participants' ability to remain calm and collected under pressure but also reinforces the significance of thorough emergency preparedness and response strategies.

Radio communication scenarios are designed to enhance participants' proficiency in standard aviation communication protocols. Through simulated ATC interactions, pilots will practice clear and concise communication, ensuring accurate transmission and receipt of flight instructions, clearances, and other essential information. This exercise highlights the critical role of effective communication in maintaining flight safety and navigating the complexities of air traffic control systems.

Navigational aids usage will be explored through hands-on exercises that challenge participants to employ various navigational tools and technologies. From traditional VOR navigation to modern GPS-based systems, participants will navigate predefined routes, demonstrating their ability to effectively use these aids to maintain course accuracy and situational awareness. This exercise emphasizes the evolving nature of aviation navigation and the need for pilots to be proficient with both traditional and contemporary navigational methods.

Decision-making in emergency situations will be further emphasized through scenarios that require quick and informed choices. Participants will be presented with complex situations where immediate decisions could mean the difference between safety and disaster. These exercises aim to sharpen the participants' ability to assess risks, prioritize actions, and implement the most appropriate response under time-sensitive conditions.

Identifying and responding to airspace infringements is another critical exercise. Pilots will work with simulated flight tracks to recognize and correct potential airspace violations before they occur. This exercise reinforces the importance of thorough pre-flight planning, continuous situational awareness during flight, and understanding the ramifications of airspace infringements.

Understanding and applying weather information in the context of flight planning and execution will be addressed through exercises that require participants to interpret advanced meteorological data. Pilots will assess the impact of weather phenomena on planned flights, making adjustments as necessary to ensure safety. This exercise not only tests weather knowledge but also emphasizes its critical impact on flight operations.

Fuel planning and management exercises will challenge participants to calculate fuel requirements accurately, considering factors such as flight distance, weather conditions, and reserve requirements. This exercise highlights the importance of meticulous fuel management in ensuring the aircraft's endurance and safety throughout the flight.

Through these comprehensive practical exercises, participants are immersed in a variety of scenarios that test their knowledge, skills, and decision-making abilities. Each exercise is designed to bridge the gap between theoretical knowledge and practical application, ensuring that aviation professionals are well-prepared to navigate the complexities of the aviation industry. By engaging in these exercises, participants will solidify their understanding of the FAR/AIM 2025, enhancing their competence and confidence in their operational roles within the national airspace system.

Made in the USA
Columbia, SC
04 December 2024

48421432R00074